How To **Reset** Your Foundations

rēStart

For A Fresh Future

Brett Johnson

rēStart

This edition published in 2020 by Indaba Publishing, a division of The Institute for Innovation, Integration & Impact, Inc.

ISBN: 978-1-947599-19-2
(e-Book)

www.brettjohnson.biz

B

rēStart: rest+art

The art of working from a place of rest.

Table of Contents

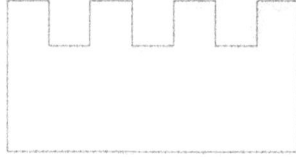

*To the people who believe
it is not over
until God says it is over.
Until then, they keep on
keeping on.*

Pre-amble

I have been talking to business owners from around the world since April 2020, and many see the Covid19 crisis as an opportunity to rethink their business. Most are considering service, not just survival. How can they better meet people's needs? Can they get rid of unprofitable products? Should they go virtual and have a greater reach? Are there opportunities closer to home? How can supply chains be reworked for good? Do they need an office at all? How can they serve their local communities better?

I also gathered leaders (via Zoom, of course) from Egypt, India, Madagascar, Nigeria, South Africa, the UK and USA and Zimbabwe to brainstorm new opportunities. I created a huge Mind Map of possibilities. This was coupled with several weeks of daily livestreaming with business leaders from around the globe looking at what you might call "eternal principles" or "ancient truths" regarding restarts. We are not the first to encounter plagues and crises.

We are, however, at a special time in history when we have had a "press pause" on business-as-usual, giving us the time to reflect on whether we want future business to look like old business. As I thought this through, it seemed there would be value in deliberately activating things we know to be true but which might be lying dormant. (During the global pandemic dormant seeds might sprout, but they may also rot.) We needed space to talk through these things and ensure we surfaced on the right side of the Red Sea.

This matter of "restart" is not just true for our careers or corporations: it is a national issue in many countries. There are people on various sides of political and social issues who are declaring "enough is enough." The outcome of social upheaval is never certain. It is crucial that the principles of restart be understood. It is as important that the platforms supporting change be legitimate; habitual adherence to parties and personalities can be dangerous. We have to examine the platforms that underpin politics to see if they align with eternal truth. We are in grave danger, as I point out in Principle #27, when we call good evil and evil good.

To explore these topics I created an online "class"—more of an activation experience, really—that tackled 12 themes. You can learn more about this in the Appendices if you like. I am not sure whether we will run the rēStart class again, but I have included snippets of feedback from participants from many nations who took part in the first two classes; their perspectives might just encourage you.

As I indicated, this book began as 50 short podcasts; I have modified them slightly for print, so if you would like to explore the audio rendition you can find them at http://brettjohnson.biz/podcast. There are follow-on seasons that should also be useful.

Every chapter in this book contains a simple principle that will hopefully inspire you as you reset foundations and restart whatever you are doing.

Brett Johnson

Brett Johnson
November, 2020

Principle # 0: God is no stranger to fresh starts

God is no stranger to the concept of restarting, and you'll find many instances in history where, in some respects, things began again. One of these is Noah where there was a reset in the Earth. There was a flood of biblical proportions, as the saying goes, and after that a fresh beginning for humanity.

You'll find that again, for the nation of Israel, as they come out of Egypt after they've been there for 430 years: this was another way to reset what happens in a nation.

Centuries later we see a prophecy about Jesus and his coming to earth in Isaiah 61, and embedded in that prophecy is Isaiah talking about the fact that Messiah will come and bring about a reset of the religious system in Israel together with massive changes in other systems. The first coming of Jesus to earth was a major reset which might pale in comparison to an upcoming reset when he returns to rule on earth.

And then you'll find there was a reset in the reign of various kings across the different eras of Israel's history, again and again, and again.

We can see by express statement and deduction that there are principles in scripture for restarting things at the personal, family, national and global level. Restarting is not something new to God. The scripture says that God is the God of new beginnings.

The question is how do we evaluate what's going on in the world? And how do we uncover these key principles? The questions are not just "Do I start this business? Do I quit this job? How do I provide?" but "What are the key underlying principles that are foundational to a reset, to a restart, to a new beginning?" It is these principles that I am sharing in this book. There are 50 short chapters or readings, if you prefer. Hopefully, you'll find them both inspirational and useful. Take two or three minutes at the beginning of your day or the end of your day. You might also find it useful to listen to the podcasts that parallel these chapters. (http://brettjohnson.biz/podcast)

My hope is that you will find more than just information and inspiration in these pages, but that you will experience activation that blows away the twin giants of passivity and paralysis.

Principle # 1: God's people are not exempt from misfortune

We are examining 50 principles for a future reset and the first principle is that God's people are not exempt from political unrest, shenanigans, things that are going on in the world. So, political misfortune impacts people, and we read in Exodus chapter 1 verses 8 to 10 that a new king, one who did not know about Joseph came to power in Egypt and said, "Look, these Israelites have become more numerous than us. They are going to be a problem. They're going to ally with our enemies, so we need to constrain them."

The whole nation was impacted by this political shift. Often we need to realize that we are part of a broader span of history and that the things that are happening to us are happening in a wider context; it is not all about us. When we have this realization we can prepare our heads and hearts giving an internal shock absorber that enables us to deal with those situations. When I grew up, if there was a crisis the typical response was, "Well, let's have a good cup of tea," or "Worse things happen when the ship goes down." This is tribute to the British background, I suppose.

Shifting into the business space, you have to have broad shoulders if you're asking God to bless you, because sometimes blessing comes with repercussions. People can be jealous of your success and, at a national level, there can be kick back.

It was the leading of God that took Jacob and sons to Egypt, but 430 years later, when a new Pharaoh was in town, their being blessed resulted in genocide and infanticide, by which I mean the killing of babies. It was a horrible situation. We have to understand that we're not exempt from the difficulties when we go through life. I'll speak later about how we can ask for a special favor: we can ask for special treatment from God. But for the moment, it's good to understand that God's people are often found in the midst of political misfortune. And this certainly has been true for the Jewish people as a nation for century after century. So, when you get into a situation and you say, "God, I want you to bless me. I want you to protect me. I want you to shield me," just bear in mind that until God breaks through, we're generally not exempt from what's going on around us.

At the time of writing there are huge race relations issues in the USA. God's people of all palettes and persuasions are part of this moment in history. We cannot hide away and say, "Oh, we are not part of the story." It is impacting the nation. As the COVID-19 crisis results in economic reverses and future advances we are all part of story. The question then becomes, "God, what are you doing in the midst of a crisis?"

Principle # 2: Adapt through crafty compassion

As I write this we are still dealing with the COVID-19 crisis. There are other issues in many places in the world: wars, food insecurity, political instability, decimated industries and more. Our principle in this chapter: Adapt through crafty compassion. We are reading in Exodus where Moses is born. As you know, there's been a decree that says all Israelite babies must be killed at birth, which is a terrible decree. The Israelite midwives do not comply with the government's decree and the babies keep getting born. They say (paraphrased), "Look the Israeli women are really tough and they pop those babies out before we can get there to kill them."

 Moses is born in this manner and his mom hides him in a basket. The mother sends the older sister off just to keep an eye on the basket, and one day, while Pharaoh's daughter is going down for a bathe in the river Nile, she hears the baby crying. Moses must have been a cute kid and we can imagine the princess saying, "Cute little baby." She wants to take the baby. Just then the savvy sister comes along and says, "Good morning, princess, can I find you somebody to nurse the baby?" "Sure", says Pharaoh's daughter. The young girl goes and gets her mom. What transpires in this crafty tale is that Pharaoh's daughter is providing incubation capital and literally an incubator for Moses Inc. She is investing in the man that's going to overcome her nation. And so, the mom adapts and takes on the role of a servant. She is not known as "mommy" but as "wet nurse" which does not sound glamorous. But, having said that, she is there with her child and Moses is spared death. From the mom's perspective, if she was open to offense, it could have been quite a humiliating situation.

You can imagine Pharaoh's daughter saying, "Oh, coochee coo. This is my son..." All the while the real mother nurses the child. And then, at the age when he's big enough, she comes and presents this boy to Pharaoh's daughter. She gives up her son, reminiscent of the Father giving up Jesus. She gives up her son. And Pharaoh's daughter names him Moses. This is an interesting situation. We have both Miriam, who is Moses' sister, and Moses' mother. Both put their life and limb at risk. They step up in a crisis and go through this tricky situation. If the princess wanted to she could have said, "Surely you must have known, surely you must be a relative, surely..." There would have been many "gotcha" situations, yet our heroines adapted through crafty compassion. I believe that at this time, if we're compassionate, we will find opportunities and then we need to match our compassion with boldness in order to see the opportunities that lie before us in this season.

Principle # 3: You often need to be in something to liberate others from it

When there is a crisis we want to be taken out of the tough situation, removed far from the difficulty. If our prayers were answered we would miss a key principle: you sometimes need to be in something in order to liberate others from it. Often you need to be in a situation if you are going to free others from it. I find people in banking systems, in the business world, in tough economic situations, in NGOs... and there are inherent or systemic problems. Until you understand what's going on in that environment it's hard to liberate others from it. So, back in Exodus, we find the boychild grew older and she, being Moses's mom, took the child to Pharaoh's daughter and he became her son. She named him Moses saying, "I drew him out of the water."

Now the very interesting question is whether this mother knew that her son would liberate the nation. Mary did. A pagan princess names a Jewish boy who would then come to know the system from which Israel would have to be liberated. Moses knew the Courts of Pharaoh because he grew up in those courts as a prince. He had a long 40 years to think about the good, the bad and the ugly of those systems. He lived and worked for many years in that Egyptian system, so he got to know how it functioned, what was good about it, what was bad about it, the inside way in which things happened, the challenges, the opportunities.

Nearly 80 years later we can look back and we see his role. Here's the point. In 2 Corinthians chapter 5 says that God has made us ministers of reconciliation. You can rarely liberate people from a system unless you've been in that system, unless you know how it works, unless you've seen it from the inside. Many people I know sit in corporate jobs or they work in government. They don't work in government because they think government is perfect. They see the flaws. They don't work in a corporate because they say, "This corporate is the be all and the end all." They see the difficulties whether they work in banking, financial services or healthcare.

During the crisis we have seen that the flaws of many of these systems are made apparent. (We cannot get drugs, masks, medical equipment, food... toilet paper!) We can either be isolationists and say, "Have nothing to do with it. We'll make our own medicines," or you can say, "I understand it. I've been there. I've seen how they work and therefore I understand their weaknesses and their strengths. I understand that from which God will need to liberate people." We often have to be in a system before we can liberate people from it. Look at your life experiences you've had, look at your past work experience, look at the systems in which you have operated and say, "What's good? What's foundationally true? What's flawed? And how do I set people free from that which is not godly, starting with myself?"

Principle # 4: God sends his people into crises

Our fourth leadership lesson on restarting: God often leads His people into a crisis. The story of God calling Moses is legendary. Moses is out in the back of nowhere minding his own business, looking after the sheep, and he sees this bush burning. It's an unusual phenomenon. He approaches it, and God tells him, to cut a long story short, "Look, I've seen the suffering of my people. I've heard their groans and their cries and I'm going to liberate them. I'm going to take them out of Egypt and take them to the Promised Land, the land of milk and honey." And Moses is thinking, "Awesome. This is great." And then God says, *"So now go, I'm sending you to Pharaoh to bring my people, the Israelites, out of Egypt."* Until then it was great news. God's going to liberate the Israelites. And then God drops one on Moses and says, "So you go."

What's the principle? God often leads us into a crisis, into a problem situation. As Western Christians, when a problem comes, we pray that God will take the problem away. As biblical believers, we should be praying that God will take us to the problems of His choosing. Not every problem is your problem. Not every giant is your giant, but the fact is you are born to fight giants. You are designed to solve problems on this planet that bother God, and He typically works through His people. So, if you understand that God sends leaders into crises then you will be more available and readier to go. It's okay to ask some clarifying questions. "Who is sending me?" God actually responds, *"Say to the Israelites the Lord, the God of your fathers, the God of Abraham, the God of Isaac and the God of Jacob has sent me to you. This is my name forever, the name by which I am to be remembered from generation to generation."*

In Exodus 3:14, God says to Moses, *"I am who I am. This is what you are to say to the Israelites. I am has sent me to you."* As God sends you into a crisis, make sure you go with the endorsement of His name. Make sure you know your identity, which we'll touch on a bit in the next chapter, but also know that you go with the endorsement of His name. God does indeed send His people into crises. It's good to know your identity, it's smart to know your calling, and it's essential to know who is sending you.

Principle # 5: You can ask for affirmation

Today we find ourselves in Exodus chapter four and Moses answered, *"What if they do not believe me or listen to me when I say 'the Lord has appeared to me'? What if they don't believe me?"* Our next principle is this: you can ask for affirmation. When God calls you into a situation, it's alright to say, "Okay, God, give me some confirmation over here. Give me some affirmation." What happens next is fascinating: God asks Moses "What's in your hand?" Moses had his shepherd's staff; it was a principle means of production or earning income. God tells him to throw it on the ground and it turns it into a serpent. If that wasn't freaky enough, God then tells Moses to pick it up again. He gingerly picks it up again by the tail.

There was more: God told Moses to put his hand inside his cloak and it comes out leprous. Moses puts it back in and comes out healed. Wow, that's quite something! These two signs are quite amazing, but they are not party tricks: signs and wonders confirm a calling, and it is within scope to ask, "God, is there some affirmation that you're going to give me as you send me on a suicide mission... What seems to be an impossible task?" His answer might be his person, as we say in the previous chapter, or it might be something supernatural. I remember when I was in my mid-twenties and leading a local church while working at a large accounting firm I would stop on my way home from work, sit on the rocks next to the ocean and call out to God to confirm his word with signs and wonders. I needed more than "faithful teaching" or "good words" – I needed God to confirm his calling with the backing of miracles.

God does confirm his words with signs and wonders. In the New Testament, Jesus said, "These signs shall accompany those who believe." We don't want to move in presumption; we want to move in faith. The flip side, however, is that when God tells us to move and we simply say it cannot be done (and we don't even bother to ask for a confirmation) that's not just a waste of resources, that's sin. If God sends us to do something and we don't do it on the presumption that we're not capable...

Here's a little secret: you're not capable. God knows you're not capable. God doesn't call you because of your capability. He calls you because he needs somebody to do a job. During a crisis situation as you observe the issues that are out there you cannot simply say, "Ah, I don't have what it takes." That's not a surprise to God. You and I don't have what it takes, but that does not get us out of the calling. When God says, "There's a problem," he typically follows with, "and I want you to get involved in solving that problem." Do not overdo the "Me, little old me, is this God really sending me?" because, while it is fine to ask for a confirmation, false humility is not pretty. False humility is actually just an inverted form of pride (another form of pride). We'll unpack that in the next chapter.

Principle # 6: God is ahead of you in the rēStart

As we explore these short biblical principles that underpin the notion of restart remember that God is way ahead of you. As your business gets reset, as you explore new opportunities, God is already looking down the road to your new future.

We find Moses still making big excuses. "I can't speak, I can't do this. I can't do that." Basically he's saying, "Look, did the email go to the wrong guy? I mean, surely you're not sending me back to Egypt. You know I blew it. You know I'm not very eloquent. You know I'm just out the octogenarian in the middle of the desert, a Midianite shepherd." That's the paraphrase.

Moses says to the Lord in an almost quaint way, *"Pardon your servant, Lord. I've never been eloquent. Neither in the past, nor since you've spoken to your servant. I'm slow of speech and tongue."*
And God says to him, *"Who gave human beings their mouths? Who makes them deaf or mute? Who gives them sight or makes them blind? Isn't it me? Is it not I, the Lord? Now go."*

So Moses tries again and says, in effect, "Thanks, God, but no thanks." *"Pardon your servant, Lord. Please send someone else."* It might be quite cute if it wasn't so serious how Moses says, "Pardon your servant, Lord. Send somebody else."

God is not that impressed with Moses' humility. He's calling you because there's a need, not because you're talented, smart, rich, spiritual, gifted, eloquent, or the best shepherd in

Midianville. He's calling you because there's a need and somebody has to do the job.

> Then the Lord's anger burned against Moses. And he said, "What about your brother, Aaron, the Levite? I know he can speak well. He's already on his way to meet you and he'll be glad to see you."

What's God saying? "Look, Moses, I suspected you might object so I've already spoken to your brother. He's on his way, he's going to be gung ho, excited to meet you."

Do not panic: God is ahead of you in this whole global pandemic with all its ramifications. He's already thought about the team you need, he's figured out the resources you need. God is expecting you and me to stop making excuses, to pack our travel bag and get on with the job that he's called us to do. Remember what we covered in the previous chapter: false humility is pride. We should not still be saying, "I'm not very good at this. I'm not very good at that," all the while waiting for God to say, "Oh no, you're awesome."

God's anger burned against Moses when he got to the point where he said, "Look, enough is enough, right? Enough of the protesting." You and I might need to look at areas in our lives where I've made excuses or delayed. Be mindful of the fact that some delays are permanent dead-ends. Open yourself to the Father's whisper, "I'm already ahead of you on this one."

Principle # 7: rēStart requires holiness

How do we get up and going again when there has been a global reset? What are some of the biblical principles that apply to the many restarts in scripture? Our next principle, principle #7, is this: restart requires holiness. By now we know that Moses decided to go, to follow God's instruction, and he is heading off towards Egypt. Moses is probably pondering his rather dramatic encounter with God. He might even have been musing on the past where God has said to him, "Tell Pharaoh 'because you wouldn't let Israel, who's my first born, go I'm going to kill your firstborn.'" Moses probably has such as this on his mind and partway to Egypt, the Lord meets him and decides he wants to kill him. That's what the scripture says in Exodus 4:24. God decided to kill Moses. Moses' wife, who was an African lady, by the way, spots the issue and intervenes on her husband's behalf by circumcising their child.

There's this principle that, in spite of the fact even that you've been obedient and you have started down the road of obeying God and following His calling, you still have to have holiness in your life. Obedience actually reveals things in our life that need to be reset. It's as we get going and we say, "Yes, God, here I am. Send me. Use me." ... as we are on the way things are surfaced that have to be dealt with. This is a time in history for us to look at things within our work or business that need to be reconsidered. Did I do that right? Was that the right kind of contract that I had? Were these the right business partners? Was I serving the right audience? Was I serving the right audience for the right reason? What were my motives like? Was I actually intent on extending the kingdom of God or just covering my bills on a monthly basis, building up my retirement?

God can give you a fresh call as you come out of this Coronavirus crisis. He can call us, and he can require that we step up and clean up our act. Interestingly, it wasn't a case of willful disobedience in the case of Moses, but the principle remains that we have to live to a new level of holiness as we follow God if we are to overcome the things that bind ourselves and others to the Egyptian system.

Another lesson here is that your spouse is sometimes... often...make that <u>usually</u>, your best ally. Therefore make sure that you stay in sync with your wife and that you are listening to what she has to say if you're a husband. If you're a wife, listen to what your husband has to say. You might not have done business together before. You might not have been on the same team. Maybe he went off to work and you were at home. Maybe you were pursuing your career and he was doing something else. Recognize that sometimes your best ally and the one who prevents God from opposing you is your spouse, the person that you're involved with on a day to day basis.

"Things have already started to move and shift in my life. I am no longer fearful of the future. I have an incredible hope. I am so excited for the future and post lockdown coronavirus economy." Dirk

---

Principle # 8: Things need to come to a head before you get ahead

We're in a time of unprecedented crisis, if not unprecedented, certainly unusual for our times. So what do we have to do in a time like this? Moses has now obeyed God. He has gone to see Pharaoh, and he's presented his somewhat audacious request that the people of Israel be allowed to go into the desert to worship God. Pharaoh has responded by saying, "Who is this Lord that you're talking about? I don't know him, and I'm not going to let your people go." Then Pharaoh doubled down on the Israelite's work requirements by going to his supervisors and saying, "Go and tell those lazy Israelites they need to make the same a number of bricks, but without straw, without hay." The Israelites are now under more pressure despite the fact that Moses and Aaron have obeyed God.

God had warned Moses and said "He's going to have a hard heart, this Pharaoh guy, so be prepared." After Moses has obeyed God the Israeli leaders come to Moses and Aaron and say, "God is going to judge you because you've bought trouble upon us." Their specific words are, *"May the Lord look on you and judge you. You've made us obnoxious to Pharaoh and his officials."* Sometimes you obey God and you appear to be obnoxious to other people. "How can this person do that? How can they do that?" Remember Lazarus when he's lying in the tomb and Jesus gets the message: "Lazarus stinks." Sometimes we obey God; we're waiting for the miracle, but there's no empty tomb yet, and we look foolish. There is sometimes a hockey stick effect, they call it in business, where you go down before you go up. The principle is clear: Often things need to come to a head before you can get ahead.

God definitely called Moses and Aaron, but things got worse. Sometimes things get worse before they get better. We're in a crisis and we don't know how the COVID-19 pandemic is going to end. There are racial issues across the U.S., there are issues of government control, perhaps overreach, and there are international complexities around China, the U.S., Russia... the list goes on. These issues are actually bigger than you and me. Our role in what God wants us to do, plus the timing of what He wants to do, is not just dependent upon us. There's something bigger at play. Keep yourself in a posture where you don't expect everything to be just awesome after you have started to obey God. You can start to obey God and things can get more difficult. That doesn't mean you should give up. Hang in there, persevere through the crisis and look for the purposes of God both in the middle of and on the other side.

"What really struck me was the number of people, the caliber of people, people who were running their own businesses, people at the C-suite level, who had a need and a desire just to be with others, inviting God to redirect them in whatever way He pleased to do.

No matter who I was thrown into a group with, three or four people, we always seemed to just be able to connect very well. We all acknowledged that it felt like we'd known each other forever. We felt a high degree of trust and wanting to help each other. I realized that I needed something like this to break into my life and get my attention. It's been life-changing. It's definitely changed my perspective and made me very hungry to collaborate with God in everything I do." –Tim

Principle # 9: Crises are opportunities to know God more fully

As Israel weathered their crisis and God was giving Moses and Aaron daily lessons in how to rēStart a nation we come to Principle # 9 where we have to answer the question, "Who is God to you?" A crisis often reveals our heart-beliefs about who God is to us personally, not academically, but in reality.

The extension of this principle is that as we go through a crisis we can experience a new level of intimacy with God, of knowing God, that we've not experienced before. Moses went to Pharaoh and it did not go well. Moses then lays out a question in the last few verses of Exodus 5.

> *Moses returned to the Lord, and said, "Lord, why have you caused trouble for this people? Why did you ever send me? From the time I went to speak to Pharaoh in your name, he has caused trouble for this people, and you have certainly not rescued them!"*

What answer would you expect to such direct questions? Here's the answer from Exodus Chapter Six.

> *"I am the Lord. I appeared to Abraham, to Isaac, and to Jacob as God Almighty, but by my name the Lord, I did not make myself fully known to them."*

God is saying to Moses, "Listen up, Moses. In the past I appeared to Abraham, Isaac, and Jacob, which is amazing, but I didn't let myself be known to them by my Name." In a crisis we want the answer to be things: revenue, cash flow, tax relief, food—and God tells us the answer is his Name. Things are not the answer. We have an opportunity in a crisis to know the Name of God and who he is to us in our career, in our life, in our business and our family in a new and intimate way.

Now, knowing the name of God in our business is bigger than God just putting in an appearance, if you like, from time to time. It is more than inviting him to our annual planning or the annual review. No, this is knowing the name of God, the character, the attributes, how God does things and why God does things so that these become ingrained, seeped into, the culture of our work and of our business. You might be an employee somewhere and you've said, "Ah, but the company doesn't allow this. The company allows that." This is a time of change. In fact, it's a time of unusual change. It's a season when you can have a voice and where your values, your principles and your truth can be lived out on a daily basis.

When we moved from South Africa to Silicon Valley in the mid-1980s few were talking about work-life integration. Friends working at Apple in 2012 tried to get me to speak there on Convergence to a group of Christians, but Apple wanted assurances I would not talk about my faith and asked to preview my slides. The talk never happened, yet today Apple , like many other companies, recognizes that their staff need to bring all of themselves, including their faith, to work. A crisis can give you a voice.

I meet many businesspeople—owners and professionals—who have let God "put in a guest appearance" in their businesses and they think they are doing him a favor. They invite him particularly when there's a problem, "God, we have a problem. Sales are down. We have an employee issue." But God says, "I want my name to be known—my character, my nature, the essence of who I am—so that when you slice through the company, in any department, any business process, any division or any location you can see my attributes." People will then say, "These are the characteristics of who God is." It's not enough to just have his name on your business card. His attributes must be fully integrated into every crevice of your organization.

A call to being a kingdom initiator is a call to knowing God more intimately. Let's not waste this time where God has pressed pause on the world. Let's ask, "God, who are you really to me? And who do you want to be in my business, in my workplace, in my career, and in my whole household? Who do you really want to be?"

"rēStart played a significant role in activating how I collaborate with God and move forward in faith into the marketplace with a viable business." —Chloe

---

Principle # 10: Discouragement blocks our ears

Things were getting exciting in Egypt. Moses was back in town after a 40-year absence and Pharaoh was beginning to take note. God spoke to Moses and said, "I've made known my name to you." And then God adds, "Go tell the people I'm going to be their God. They're going to be my people." Moses goes to the people but when he gets there the people can't hear it. Why? Let's listen to it from Exodus Chapter Six.

> *"Moses reported this to the Israelites, but they did not listen to him because of their discouragement."*
> *Exodus 6:9*

When we're discouraged it's hard for us to hear God speak to us. It is crucial in these seasons that we figure out how we can stay in a place of encouragement. What can we do to keep ourselves encouraged? Here are some quick pointers. First, avoid the news. Yes, you can know what's going on, but don't spend endless time watching CNN, CBN, Fox News, BBC or whatever your news source is. Beware that an onslaught of negative news can impact your ability to hear God. Why? Because a daily diet of bad news will make you discouraged. When we're discouraged, we get beans in our ears, as my mother used to say, we get things that block our hearing and our listening. (By the way, it is not just the information communicated but the spirit behind it that is intent on sowing confusion and despair in our lives.)

Second, make sure that you don't get stuck under circumstances. We have to keep momentum at this time.

Third, another way to keep yourself encouraged is to get enough sleep. Don't fill your time with trivial things that rob you of adequate rest.

Fourth, read the Word of God. A friend of mine, Iain Muir, bumped into Brother Andrew (known as God's Smuggler) on a plane and they happened to be sitting next to each other. Iain asked Brother Andrew, "How do you keep yourself encouraged? How do you deal with pressure?" He said, "I take time alone. I sleep. And I read the Word of God." It was mid-February and Brother Andrew had already read the entire scripture, cover to cover, more than twice in six weeks.

When last did I do that? Have I ever done that? Encourage yourself. "David encouraged himself in the Lord his God." Keep yourself upbeat because if you're not encouraged it's hard to hear God speak a proactive word for the future. You cannot be enshrouded in the fear of this plague or that virus and hear God.

"I feel that [reStart] gives me the space and grace to fight some personal giants. Having space to do this gives me my joy back." —Shirleen

Principle # 11: You're never too old to rēStart

Our principle for this chapter is, you're never too old to restart. Exodus 7:7 states that the combined age of the startup leadership team was 163 years... and there were only two of them. Moses was 80 and Aaron was 83 years old. Don't be tricked into thinking that you're too old to restart.

"This is just one crisis, too many. One financial collapse, too many. And we're just going to give up." I recently watched a documentary of a couple who had left the UK and gone to Croatia, bought an old stone farm house, but it had no running water, no electricity, and it was a wreck. To add to their misery the local officials had not given them building permits. The husband said, "If we don't get our planning permission, I'm just going to go back to the UK and live in a Council House," which means live rent free. He said, "I won't even come out of the front of the house to mow the lawn." (His wife said, "I think you will.") The point is we can feel like the remodeling couple in Croatia: if there's one more crisis, we don't have it in us to begin again.

We need to remember that the New Israel startup team was 80 plus 83. Isn't that pretty amazing? I remember when I was in a church in Redwood City, California and there was a man in my Convergence class who was a retired medical doctor. He said, "I've been in this church 49 years. I've occupied just about every position. I'm 80 years old, but I just believe God has something else for me." That's the attitude we need to have. We are never too late to start over.

I recently watched Sid Roth, the TV host who has shows about the miraculous, and he had just had a dream. He said,

"I'm nearly 80 years old and I'm trusting that God has more for me." Moses lived until 120 years old. His eyes weren't dim, he didn't need reading glasses. His strength didn't fade because he lived in the presence of God and stayed true to the assignment of God.

This is a time for us to watch our mental attitude. When another friend of mine turned 50 the devil whispered to him, "You've peaked. It's all downhill from here." Watch out for the lies of the enemy that tell you it's too late, it's over, you just need to retire. While the way you do things can change in different seasons in life there's no such thing as retirement in scripture, from what I see. God can take you from being a young man, to being a father, to being an old man and that's a good progression. I have no issue with that, but watch your mindset. Remember, you're never too old to restart.

We live in an era where age is disdained in some communities. Sometimes young leaders have too much to lose, however, and the older leaders... they've already lost it ,and they know they've lost it, so they don't care about their reputation. They do not worry as much about their finances; they're willing to risk more. We need more older leaders who are godly and going for it!

Maybe this is a time when the wisdom of the elders can take hands with the energy of youth. If you're young, find somebody with gray hair or no hair. If you're old, find some young people who can lift your arms, walk with you... not to serve your vision, but where collectively you can serve the kingdom together. We're looking for a multi-generational collaboration. "I am the God of Abraham, Isaac and Jacob" and later Joseph, then eventually Moses. If you've bought the lie that your years are spent and you're destined for the front porch, dust off your hat and get back on the horse. You're never too old to restart.

A rēStart Story: Susan Hill

Overworked, alone and not realizing I was wandering in the desert whilst knowing it was breakthrough to the Promised Land time. rēStart did just that! It was as if Holy Spirit came like a flood and fine-tuned things. It was like the disciples who went back to fishing when Jesus ascended. I was sliding down the slippery slope of "oh well!" Fed up, frustrated and about to ditch passion on the side of the road. Being reminded of my Kingdom focused purpose statement, identity and purpose called me back to the core of who I am and led me through the desert to the verge of Promised Land where I stand now at a Crossroads: Keeping on doing what I am doing at iKhaya [my place of work] where it's not that hard to cope with the fundraising and cultural challenges that block my entrepreneurial side or, Get vulnerable, follow God with me living an integrated life. There was a dire need to demystify the confusion and I couldn't do it alone. Having others speak into my life was encouraging and supportive, compelling me forward the way the Kingdom should! If my household wasn't buying it, then I hadn't done a good enough job with integration and I needed to dig deeper; I put this into practice straight away. As I did so I discovered there are disciples in the business whereby God's image is glorified. It's not about the specific prayer or program of salvation - it's truly about an integrated lifestyle which we've known all along. I have now found the food that fuels us - it's beyond the one man at the front, whether it be church, or NGO, or ministry. It's about making disciples, showing them the way, John 17! And we don't have to apologize for it! Being in the [prayer] quad sharpened my gifts and God-given abilities which encouraged me to speak into others' lives and to find life in the words they spoke to me! COVID 19 has given us this opportunity to anticipate, cast vision and plan for God's glory to be manifest first in what I'm doing now and in setting the foundation for going further to the making of disciples who contribute, mold and shape their township economy. They will rebuild the ancient ruins and the places long devastated - IT IS FOR SUCH A TIME AS THIS - RIGHT NOW.

These baby steps are like how babies learn to walk, but ours are about learning to walk in Kingdom Principles and Practices. It is why God extricated us. Like Nehemiah, we have seen the world's systems are not working. I truly believe God will be glorified by us walking in Kingdom principles and values in an integrated lifestyle, His image exalted and society transformed. Yes, we are still willing to go for Him - no longer afraid, no longer smarting from the wounded-ness but realizing it was preparation, qualifying and training.

Principle # 12: Reluctant follower to co-laboring leader

We see in our next batch of principles that you progress from being a reluctant follower, to an obedient person, to somebody who's co-laboring with God. Let's unpack these stages of leadership development in the life of Moses.

Setting the scene, there has been a plague of frogs and Pharaoh came to Moses and said, "Pray to the Lord to take the frogs away from me and my people and I'll let your people go to offer sacrifices to the Lord." Moses then says an interesting thing which reveals his growth as a leader. *"I leave to you the honor of setting the time for me to pray for you and your officials."* So Moses respectfully says, "Okay, great. I will pray, but you tell me the time you would like the frogs to leave." Pharaoh then gives Moses a set time.

After the interchange with Pharaoh Moses goes and cries out to God, "God, you heard what he said and I committed us to an outcome. I need you to step up and to partner with me." Again, observe the progression from being somebody who's reluctant, to somebody who's obedient, to somebody who is now learning the collaboration between man and God. What an awesome responsibility. Don't miss this subtle shift.

When you're a new believer you tend to ask, "God, what do you want me to do?" As you mature as a follower of Jesus, He wants to know what you have in mind. "What do you want to do?" There's an interesting phrase in the letter of 2 Thessalonians where Paul speaks about their persecution and suffering, but then goes on: "And we pray that by his power all the pleasures of goodness and all works inspired by faith would fill you completely." You come to a point in your development, as you restart, where God seems to be asking, "Since your goal is goodness and faith, what do you want to do? It's not just what I want. What do you want to do with the rest of your life? What do you want to do with the next season?"

The answer to such a profound invitation cannot just be "Survival" or, "Just provide for my family." We have to say, "Father God, what's on Your heart? What is Your passion for me? What's Your purpose for me? Here I am, send me." And then we have to co-labor with God, learning to collaborate with Him. We also have to unpack what it is that He's put within us. We have to activate the gifts and stir up the deposits that are within us so that we don't just get onto the same treadmill again but follow a path that God has ordained for us to walk. So, moving from reluctance to co-laboring is key. God wants us as a partner, not as a puppet.

Proverbs 25: 2 says, *"It's the glory of God to conceal a matter. To search out that matter is the glory of kings."* You're a king. You're a queen. We are sons and daughters, and it's our divine privilege to seek out what it is that God has for us. When we do this, we anticipate not just steps of obedience, but a path of co-laboring with God.

"The biggest takeaway I received from rēStart has been that I am a co-collaborator with God and He really wants me to work alongside with Him, not just for him, in accomplishing His Kingdom purposes." —
John C.

Principle # 13: rēStart requires discernment

The principle for this short chapter is this: restart requires discernment. Why does a new beginning require discernment? Not every new initiative is powered from a legitimate source. We see that when Moses and Aaron went and performed the miraculous in front of Pharaoh, Pharaoh's magicians by their own secret arts conjured up similar miracles or sometimes even the same miracle. It is not beyond the world's magicians to fake a rescue from this crisis: *"Each man threw down his staff and the staffs became snakes,"* it says in Exodus 7:12.

The magicians did the same things that Moses and Aaron did by their secret arts. They also made frogs come upon the land of Egypt in Exodus 8:7. There can be an imitation of that which is really God. As I write this we are living in a world where healthcare experts are proclaiming every week, "Oh, here's what is really going on." The reality is that they are learning as they go. People in the media and governors of states piously claim "We're doing this based on science" and imply "not hocus pocus, not faith" but it's often a science that they don't even really understand.

Economists are predicting a bounce back. It's going to be a V shape, it's going to be a hockey stick, it's going to be a W. They don't really know. They're guessing and hoping. Egypt had magicians and priests; in the world today there are people who claim to do things but without the power of God. This is the essence of the World System, namely, how to live life without having to rely on the power of God. The kingdom of God is different from this. We must have discernment. We have to know what God is saying, because we can only proceed into the new season based on what God says and who God is. We must know what scripture says, the character of God, the nature of God, plus know his rhema word—His spoken word—to us today. To hear God's word, then, not only do we have to have courage, but we also have to have discernment.

The good news is that the scripture goes on to say, "But Aaron's staff swallowed up their staffs." At the end of the day there is only one truth. Jesus Christ is King of Kings and Lord of Lords. He is not anybody's fool. And while people with an agenda are spreading fear that is fueling the Coronavirus, fomenting racial hatred that's stirring a brother against brother and fellow human beings against each other, and cooking up an economic crisis which might yet be coming... while all of this is going on we have to say, "He is the Truth, He is the King of Kings, He is the Lord of Lords." We have to fix our eyes on him, the author and the finisher of our salvation so that, as we go through these times, we're not tossed from this side to that side but have clear discernment, our feet on the ground and our eyes upon Jesus.

Principle # 14: God limits the power of your opposition

In the previous chapter we talked about the fact that restarting requires discernment. Today's principle is this: God ultimately limits the powers of magicians. What happened in Exodus Chapter 8:18, *"But when the magicians tried to reproduce the gnats by their secret arts, they could not."* Now, a gnat isn't as big as a frog. It's not as big as a snake. It's not a huge thing. It's a tiny little thing. Here in Tennessee, I am getting to know no-see-ums. (I am not making this up: According to Wikipedia, Ceratopogonidae is a family of flies commonly known as no-see-ums, or biting midges, generally 1–3 mm in length. The family includes more than 5,000 species, distributed worldwide, apart from the Antarctic and the Arctic.) These are bugs so tiny, you can't even find them, but you feel them! I go outside and I think it's a lovely day, and next thing I know is I've got pink spots on my body that itch for the next three weeks.

The magicians of Egypt couldn't reproduce the gnats, and what they concluded was, *"This is the finger of God."* Ultimately, God will not just come through, but triumph. The question will be, "Are we going to be in a posture of faith, a posture of alertness, a posture of readiness, or are we going to get duped into stillness and mediocracy and not be ready for the next thing that God is going to do?" This is a serious question. We have to see that there's a battle in the heavenlies. This whole Coronavirus crisis is not just a medical battle and it is not just an economic battle. There is at least a parallel spiritual battle. God was clearly doing amazing things on Planet Earth in late 2019 and early 2020. Stadiums were being filled, people were gathering. It now seems there has been an attempt of the enemy to block what God is doing in the world.

The question is whether we just going to take it, roll over and say, "It is just the way it is," or are we going to remember the lessons of the Israelites in Egypt? When God stepped in and said, "I'm going to do something," there was a backlash not just from Pharaoh, but from the pit of hell. There's a backlash against God's people and the move of God in the Earth. It is time for us to rise up, and it is time for us to be committed to the cause of Christ. It's time for us to be counted. Scripture says in Psalm 110:3 *"Your troops will be willing on the day of your battle."* Who is this talking? This is a conversation between Father God and King Jesus that David, the psalmist, sees through a window into heaven.

> *The Lord said to my Lord, "Sit at my right hand until I make your enemies a footstool."*

So, Father God says to Jesus, "Sit at my right hand," and then it goes on to say, "Your troops will be willing on your day of battle." This is a time to be a ready and willing troop, not to be locked down to the point of inactivity with a resulting slothfulness. Even though we may have been physically isolated, in our hearts we must remain ready to get out there. You might be thinking that you would like to go shopping, to the beach, to a restaurant, or to get your hair cut. Just like you're ready to get out and go to the store or get some exercise at the gym, so we have to be eager for the next season that God has for us. That season is not just self-preservation or economic stability but a season to advance the Kingdom. Let us come to the same conclusion, "This is the finger of God."

Pray for God's finger in your own situation: your own household, work, business, enterprise, and sphere of influence.

Principle # 15: Spiritual distancing is integral to restarting

During the Covid-19 pandemic there has been lots of discussion about social distancing and the conclusion is that it generally helps curb the spread of the virus. All around the world we are familiar with the concept, if not the practice, of social distancing: keep six feet away, seven feet away, 13 feet away, three feet away... the recommended distance varies. We've become used to this notion of keeping a space between us and others. This segment deals with a similar concept, namely, spiritual distancing. Moses insisted on it, but Pharaoh didn't favor it.

After the plagues of frogs and gnats and flies, Pharaoh calls Moses into his office and says, "Okay, you can go and worship, but you must worship here in this land. You don't need to go all the way out into the desert." But Moses says, "Pharaoh, we need to go a three-day journey from here. We need spiritual distancing because when we do our sacrifices, it's going to be detestable to your people and they're going to kill us."

There are a couple of principles here. First, when the enemy starts to get on the back foot and you're getting close to having a victory the enemy will try to get you to compromise. "Well, follow God, but just not that much. You can worship God, but you know, don't go overboard. Just keep it in moderation." Scripture records Pharaoh's proposition as a lesson for us because it is the same issue we will face when we want to get serious with God. "I will let you go to offer sacrifices to the Lord your God in the desert, but you must not go very far." I have met well-meaning people who say, "Yes, you can serve God with your business, but don't go very far, don't take it overboard." I gave a talk once at a business forum on Marketplace Miracles and how we can fight giants with inspired innovation. Afterwards the Christian professor who had invited me said words to the effect of, "I liked your talk, but I wish you had said that the businessperson developed the product after hours of research, not based on a revelation from God." Even Christians want to keep God in a safe box, worshipping him on their terms.

Jesus says to his disciples in Mark 6:32, "*Come ye yourselves apart into a desert place, and rest a while,*" in an old translation. "Come ye apart..." Sometimes we need to have a spiritual distancing in order to recharge our batteries, regroup our team, and rebuild our foundation.

Are there other reasons we might need spiritual distancing? Is it possible that we've become too close to this world, to Wall Street, to exercise, to tolerance, to political correctness? Have we made religions of things that are not true religions? Had we come to a point in early 2020 when fashion, entertainment, sports or our own image management had become too much of a thing? As humankind we have become so preoccupied with ourselves that we probably needed a divine reset—not that God caused the virus, but he can use it as a "Press Pause" on society. We need to get spiritual distancing because our 20th Century gods are deadlier than the coronavirus.

There are also things that we've tolerated in our lives that are just not acceptable to God. Epidemics of racism, sexism, ageism, denominationalism, tribalism, determinism (the right to decide who lives and dies at the hands of medical professionals) and a bunch of other "-isms" that are just not acceptable to God still abound. We need to get distanced from these things. We need some mileage—not an hour or a day, as Pharaoh proposed, but three days distance—between ourselves and these things. They have to be far from us as we head into the next season. We need spiritual distancing.

Recognize that when we let things that are not of God seep from society into our pores until they become part of our identity it is sometimes harder to detect than a virus. Let this season of social distancing remind us that we need to embrace spiritual distancing. "You are in the world, but you are not of the world. Come apart," says Jesus. I am not advocating isolationism where God-followers create and hide in holy pods. Not at all. A group of infected people hiding away together are no less infected. We need both the cleansing of the blood of Jesus to remove that which is not right and the renewal of our thinking so that we don't relocate our same mess from Egypt, via the desert, to the Promised Land.

Principle # 16: Don't expect to be treated kindly

When we are determined to reset our foundations and re-chart the course of our new future we shouldn't expect the world systems to be kind to us. Don't expect Egypt to wave you a fond farewell. Restart is about getting into a new and better system of doing things. Incumbent systems will kick and scream to keep things the way they are just as Pharaoh did because the status quo is wired to their advantage. This happens in politics. It happens in economics. One of the reasons there are racial tensions is that there are incumbent systems that kick and scream when people try to get out of their economic bondage, for example. In political systems, when somebody comes in to wreck a current system that mainly serves the incumbents well, the old guard don't roll over easily. In the banking systems, financial products are sometimes set up to enslave people through debt and excessive credit card interest, to give another example.

Old systems don't give up easily when a new system comes into town. Don't expect the world systems to be kind to you when you decide to leave. You can anticipate a fight, and don't expect it to be fair or clean. Exodus 8:32. "*But this time also Pharaoh hardened his heart and would not let the people go.*"

Exodus 9:7 says "*Pharaoh investigated and found that not even one of the animals of the Israelites had died.*" There was a plague of the animals, but not one died on the Israeli side of the cattle fence. "*Yet his heart was unyielding and he would not let the people go.*" So, there's a promise—your future is going to be better—but Pharaoh's intention was to keep the Israelites in bondage. You can bet your last dollar that the intention of the World System is to keep you in bondage.

In Exodus 9:27, after there had been a plague of hail, Pharaoh summoned Moses and Aaron, and said, *"This time I've sinned."* He said to them, *"The Lord is in the right. And I, and my people are in the wrong."* It was mostly Pharaoh that was in the wrong, by the way. "Pray to the Lord because we've had enough of thunder and hail, and I will let you go and you won't have to stay any longer." When Pharaoh saw that the rain and the hail and the thunder had stopped, however, he sinned again and changed his mind. The systems of this world are not going to let you go easily. If you're going to get out of doing things the old way and you're going to move into the Kingdom way then you need to recognize that it's going to have to be deliberate. You're going to have to think about what kind of system you want to be in in the future. What kind of business do you want to have? How are you going to operate financially? Don't just go back to business as usual, because you will have wasted a crisis. Think about the systems that you want to leave and the systems to which you want to proceed. And remember, it's going to take a fight to get out of the current system.

PS: In a book titled Repurposing Capital I compare and contrast the economic systems of Egypt, The Desert and The Promised Land. Egypt and The Promised Land are diametrically opposed on many fronts. We discuss this in the rēStart class as well.

I tried to attend every course I could in an intellectual level. But I was hit with roadblocks over the last 10 years. And then I realized, with the principles that you teach comes the spiritual force also. And then there is also another spiritual force that opposes the principles of the kingdom. When you operate in the principles of God, the angels of God are activated to help you. And the Holy Spirit of God is there to assist you. But there's also another spirit that opposes you.—John S.

Principle # 17: ultimately God's Word breaks through

In principle #16, we recognized that you shouldn't expect the world's systems to be kind to you as you might have to leave with them kicking and screaming as you go. Today the principle is this: ultimately God's Word breaks through. When Moses and Aaron went to see Pharaoh there was a whole entourage with him. They saw what happened day after day. What we notice in Exodus 9 is Pharaoh's officials beginning to observe that something is changing. Pharaoh doesn't look like God after all. It seems like there's a bigger God in town.

These officials began to turn, and it records in Exodus 9: 20, *"Those of Pharaoh's officials, who feared the word of the Lord...."* So, a growing number of Pharaoh's officials were fearing what Moses and Aaron were going to say next, what they were going to do next, and what was going to happen in the nation as a result of what these prophets pronounced. They gave a warning about hail and thunder and lightning and Moses said, "You better get your stuff inside because otherwise it's going to be trashed." And those who feared the word of the Lord hid their livestock inside. And those that didn't: their goods were finished, flattened.

> *Those of Pharaoh's servants who feared the Lord's message hurried to bring their servants and livestock into the houses, but those who did not take the Lord's message seriously left their servants and their cattle in the field.*

What happens? Ultimately, the Word of God, which is quick, powerful, sharper than any two-edged sword... it breaks through. Scripture says, "My word does not return to me void." We therefore live as people who go back and remind ourselves, "What has God spoken? What has He said? What has His Word actually stated?" The psalmist says, *"One thing God has spoken, two things I have heard."* That's pretty amazing. God said one thing; he heard two things. What was it that he heard? The two things he heard were, *"You, O, Lord are good, and you, O, Lord, are strong."* You are good, and you're strong. What did God say? In the beginning of the psalm God says, *"You will not be shaken."* (Psalm 62)

Some things are being shaken so that the unshakeable can remain. When your world is being rocked remember that eventually the word of God breaks through. Stand up every day and say, "God, I'm expecting your word to be true for me today. Some things will get fattened and some things will get flattened, and I plan to be on the side of the things that get fat, not flat. I want to be like Pharaoh's officials who fear the Word of the Lord. I want to hear your spoken word to me today. I want to revere your written word today which is alive, powerful by your Spirit."

Eventually the word of God has sway. Put yourself in the tornado line, if you like, of the Word of God, so that He can strip away that which can be stripped and shake that which will be shaken so that you are left with solid future-building materials.

Principle # 18: Giants—put a hole in their wallet

Those who have been around the Repurposing Business community for any length of time will know that we advocate using business to tackle giants. The idea is that businesses are a force for the upliftment of society as they directly tackle social ills as part of their core business. Here's a tip, in terms of today's principle: when you fight a giant, make sure you hit their pocketbook. When you tackle a hulk make sure that you put a hole in their wallet.

You'll remember William Wilberforce when he and the Clapham Community were trying to get the abolition of slavery passed through the British parliament they tagged a rider onto a trade bill. In our case, we see Moses dealing with Pharaoh and there's been a plague of hail. Scripture says is that the flax and barley crops were destroyed since the barley had headed and the flax was in bloom. The wheat and the spelt, however, were not destroyed because they ripened later.

The plague of hail wasn't just to put dents in people's trucks and cars, it was actually to hit the opponents of the Jews economically. In response to the economic blow Pharaoh said, "Okay, okay, I've sinned. I'll let the people go." Now, he didn't let the people go, but there's still this important principle that if you want to tackle a giant it's a good idea to rattle their economic systems.

You see, Egypt had cheap, free, slave labor and they were using it for all sorts of government projects some of which you might call "vanity projects" – building these big memorials for Pharaoh and his team. The hail and the previous plagues were messing with their economy. By the time we get to Exodus 10 some aspects of the economy had been hobbled, but there were still some sectors left standing. What comes up next was the swarming locusts, and Moses warned, "They're going to devour whatever little you have left."

What were Moses and Aaron doing? They were saying, "We are going to mess with your economy. We're going to make it so uncomfortable for you because we're going to ravage your sources of income and jeopardize your future provision." If you want to restart you sometimes need to wreck the enemy's economic models and put a hole in the pocketbook of giants.

In the hidden battle of this crisis this still happens through different types of taxes or various forms of legislation. It happens through aid to failing entities that have a sting in the economic tail. (Surely you have seen during the global pandemic that laws have been made that hamper the ability of some to "do business until I come" as Jesus commanded. Churches have been closed, storefronts shuttered, whole industries stopped dead in their tracks. Others have sprung up and profited from the new normal.)

You and I need to have a counter-movement and need to be asking, "God, are there some things that I can do differently in the economics of my business that would bring about a change and create a freedom for your people, things that would let your people go? Are there elements I can change in my industry or in my particular business that would undermine the strongholds of the enemy and hit the giant in the pocketbook?"

Principle # 19: Your enemy won't be rational

We go to Exodus Chapter 10 for the next principle. Pharaoh's officials said to him, *"How long will this man be a snare to us? Let the people go so that they may worship the Lord their God. Do you not yet realize that Egypt is ruined."* The principle is simple: your enemy is not going to be rational. Pharaoh's advisors are beginning to think, "This Moses codger has become a snare to us, and now he's promising a plague of locusts like we've never seen before." Despite this realization there's a principle: you cannot rationalize with the enemy. The demonic is neither rational, nor reasonable, but personal and vindictive. Pharaoh did not realize, period. This restart concept is not just about how you get your business going again, but how do you get your business out of Egypt, through the desert, and into the Promised Land.

This book is not designed to help you re-establish your River Nile Sunset Cruise business. I am not just trying to restart a bakery in downtown Cairo. We want to set up a kosher bakery enterprise in the Promised Land and to do that we have to get out of Egypt. To get out of Egypt, which generally refers to this world's economic system and slavery to this world's system, we have to recognize that the system will try to keep us there, dependent upon it and not dependent upon God. It will therefore do even irrational things to enslave us and to keep us trapped.

This season is about God versus Satan, not about whether your business survives another meltdown or difficulty, or who will win the next election. This therefore means we have to view this season from a spiritual perspective, not just from a practical place. "God, what's going on? What's happening in the nations? What's happening in the economies of the world? How can I align my business? How can my business be a resource that's ready for you?" I am shocked by the perfunctory understanding many Christians have about the behind-the-scenes spiritual dynamics of this time. In Egypt it was "in your face" sorcery and magicians. Today polished politicians spew vitriol and propose policies that can come from nowhere other than the pit and Christians are none the wiser.

One of the people that I like in Scripture is John the Baptist. What an amazing assignment he had and part of his job was to prepare the nation of Israel for the coming of Christ. Part of your job and my job is to use our work which can take us to the nations to prepare for the return of the Lord Jesus Christ. And so, when we are looking at this crisis, we have to say, "God, what are you doing in the world?" Do not expect to negotiate rationally with that which wants to entrap us in the current system of Egypt's economy. Don't expect to be let go easily. And don't expect your enemy to be rational because this is personal: it's between God and Satan, and we're watching it play out in history.

Principle # 20: Anticipate special treatment from God

I'm going to track back a little bit in Exodus to look at a key principle: It's okay to ask God for special treatment. In Exodus 8:23 scripture says, *"I will make a distinction between my people and your people."* It can be different for us. We can say the sun shines down on everybody, the rain comes down on everyone, but we can also ask for a distinction. We can ask God to protect our family from the plague, from the famine, from the disease and from any economic catastrophe that might be looming.

In Chapter 9:6, Pharaoh looks out after there's been the plague of the hail and he sends his investigators to find out what's happened to the animals of the Israelites. You know what he finds? Not even one of the animals of the Israelites had died. Not one. You can ask God for special treatment.

As a believer you stand upon the word of God. You have faith in the unseen God and that has advantages. That's what our confidence is based on. It isn't in a vaccine. It's not in some magical remedy or cure. Our confidence is in God. We can stand without fear of the Coronavirus or other issues because we depend upon God and we stand on his word. Ask God for special treatment as an underscoring of his interest in, his investment in, your business and as an underscoring of his goodness, not as an act of presumption, but just an appeal to his benevolence and who he is.

You can proclaim, "The plague shall not come near me. I won't have smoke on my clothes. Not one hair on my head will be missing. None of my animals will die. None of my customers will go away."

To be clear, I do know businesses that have already closed because of this crisis. Sometimes it's an opportunity to prune what we should actually get rid of today for future fruitfulness. We can pare things back, we can be more focused... and we can also say to God, "God, give me special treatment. I'm your child and I don't want one of my animals to die."

Remember father Abraham, the father of our faith, that he believed God was the God "who gives life to the dead and calls things that are not as though they are." Bring your business, bring your enterprise, bring your household and your work before God at this time and say, "God, I'm your kid and I'm asking you for special favor, for special treatment. It's not what I deserve, but it's because of your goodness and your greatness."

Intercede on behalf of your household before a good God.

A rēStart story: Hannes Visser

God's Grace & Miracles at Sennah Handling Systems
(27 April 2020, Paarl, South Africa)

As I can remember the year of 2019 as a year of absolute grace, 2020 unfolds as a year of miracles. As South Africa entered the lockdown period on 26 March 2020, our company had already paid out its last funds towards wages and salaries for the February month end. Our financial lockdown had started in January 2020 already following six years of struggle after a record year in 2013.
It was extremely hard for us to send our workers into lockdown without money to pay their salaries. God provided some parts sales that we could cover the rent of those that had no savings to fall back on. Some we helped with a bit of money for food, each time drawing the bank account to the maximum.

Our State President made mention of donations and government funds to help small businesses, but due to a previous financial crisis our company was not up to date with its taxes and does therefore not comply with the applications for these help schemes. We applied for a compromise with SARS previously, but every time there was cash in the bank, they did not respond, and when they responded, that cash had been used to pay salaries.

I got the idea to contact the South African tax authority, SARS, during the second week of the lockdown and ask of them to write off our tax debt as a way of helping us as a small business. Our accountant immediately said that that is not SARS policy and he would not even try. I got the name of someone in the Christian community who worked at SARS for years and contacted him straight away. I heard the same from him as our accountant had said. SARS will not write off your debt unless your company was liquidated. He asked if I did not have the money to offer a compromise to SARS. We had no money in the bank to offer SARS. The man commented that if this was the case, our business was dead already, and that we may as well liquidate and do business in another form or entity.

The idea of liquidating the company and coming out debt free was short lived. We realized that all our earthly possessions were linked to the business and even so, if we wanted to continue in this same kind of business, we would have to buy our equipment back out of the liquidation with money we do not have. We would also be dishonoring our debt to our creditors who, themselves are struggling. I was reminded of the passage in Hebrews 12 that I read that very morning. Esau sold his birth right for food. Having done that, he never got the chance to repent. He could never make things right again. I knew this scripture from a previous time but was just caught off guard with this opportunity to become debt free.

Well, if the business could not be liquidated, and was declared dead, the only thing that remained was asking God, who could revive the dry bones in Ezekiel, to revive our company. In this we had to trust the Lord with all our heart and lean not on our own understanding. This took a weekend of prayer and fasting, deliberately clearing our minds of our own plans. Sunday night I felt to tell God what I am trusting Him for. I trusted him for a business with an annual turnover of R20M per year.

In the meantime, we applied for an on-line letter of exemption to do essential business, as we supply machines for farmers. Our office would be running with skeleton staff and the workshop closed as we could not get, nor afford parts to finish the one machine we had on the floor.

As I went to the office that Monday morning, I learned that a farmer had paid for two bagging machines that he ordered a while ago. This was such a blessing, but not enough to reopen the workshop. I then remembered the names of two other clients who were contemplating to buy machines. I called them both, and both responded with orders and deposits. We could reopen.

Before lockdown we had an enquiry from Australia for our machines. It was in this same week they requested a pro forma invoice for four units. We are trusting that the Australian market will now open for our equipment and God will give us favor there.

The week before lockdown my wife and I rushed up country to do some urgent adjustments to a farmer's machines before their harvest started. Another farmer insisted in seeing us before we went home again, and the country went into lockdown. He challenged us to design a high-speed machine based on our already used design principles and challenged us to do it for only twice the cost of our existing machine. This would be to counter the costs of expensive machines imported from Europe at the high exchange rates we are now paying. We accepted the challenge, only with his word to take one machine if the design looked right to him. Early the next morning on our way home, we heard a prophesy saying that God will show His children new designs and open new business opportunities in this time of the corona virus. We could testify to that as we just received such an opportunity the night before.

The next week and still at home with the lockdown, I started the design in rough sketches on paper and sent them to our draughtsman, then working from home. We communicated with our cell phones and pictures, until we could open the office with the essential goods permit.

To cut a long story short, with 30 days of lockdown behind us, God provided us with so much hope. He also provided confirmed orders for five bagging machines, a new design that we were able to quote on already, and possible orders and an overseas market that was closed to us in the past.

The God we serve is a faithful God. In times like these we could only rely on our experience of a God that carried us through the last years and the One that gives us His promises in His Word. As king David said: "I was young and yet am old, but never have I seen the righteous forsaken or his children seeking bread".

PS.
As I proofread this the one customer called and increased his order from two bagging machines to four. God is so good to us!

Principle # 21: God's work is 100% complete

There are many stones that go into our foundations. The principles we are examining are the building blocks or base elements of a resetting or restarting of our business, our work, our household, or our enterprise. This chapter takes us to principle # 21. We need to get this deep into our belief system: God's work is complete. In the book LEMON Leadership, I talk about five types of leaders; Luminaries, Entrepreneurs, Managers, Organizers, and Networkers. (See lemonleadership.com for more on this topic.) The type of leader that gets stuff done 100 percent is the Manager. Well, in Exodus we see God the Manager at work. When they had the plague of flies and Moses prayed that the flies would go the scripture says "not one fly remained." I've been to Egypt and I appreciate this miracle because there are plenty of flies in Egypt, as there are in other countries. Here we see in Exodus 8:31 the Lord doing what Moses asked. The flies left Pharaoh and his officials and his people. Not a fly remained.

When God does a work in your business, it's a complete work. Don't ask God for a half-baked fix to your business. Come to him and say, "God... God the Manager, I want you to look at everything I'm attempting to do. I want you to look at my work. I want you to look at what's going on in my life and my career. I want you to do a complete work." Of course, the ultimate complete work was the work of Jesus Christ at Calvary when he said, "It is finished." Paul said, "I have fought the fight. I have finished the race." He's done what needs to be done, a complete work. God works on our behalf and it's a complete work. Not a one animal was injured, I mentioned earlier. God's restart is not half-baked. Expect God to be very specific with you and quite complete in his actions on your behalf.

I sat down a few nights ago and wrote out some goals for the week. I had a lot of things to do and as I pondered the long list I felt God say to me, "A goal is not a plan." Your goal might be, "No flies remaining in my business." Your goal might be, "I want to get out of Egypt," but you have to translate the goal into a plan. You have to say, "Okay, that's an aspiration, but this is where I need perspiration." As I alluded to in the introduction, rēStart principles include learning to work from a place of rest. This is important. It is also crucial that we still have to have some semblance of a plan for where we're going to go. You have to see, "Yes, that is my goal, and I am going to co-labor with God to clear the ground and level the field between where I am now and where God wants me to be." Sometimes our "stuff" gets in God's way... we have too many flies on us.

God does his work 100%, and we want to show up fully so that he can co-labor with us in that 100% effort. Remember, when God delivers us, when he frees us, when he redeems you and me, he does a 100% job. You can count on him for that, and he wants you to co-labor with him in an all-in way.

Principle # 22: Do something unusual

Today we are turning to principle number 22 which is this: Sometimes restart requires doing something unusual.

> *"Then the Lord said to Moses and Aaron, take handfuls of soot from a furnace and have Moses toss it in the air in the presence of Pharaoh."*

That's pretty weird. Go into the furnace, get some black soot, toss it up in the air in front of Pharaoh. It'll become fine dust over the whole land of Egypt, and festering boils will break out on men and animals throughout the land.

This is not logical. This is not normal. This is Moses doing what we would call today a "prophetic act." Now, I'm not very prophetic in terms of speaking out (as are some of my good friends) but God sometimes requires me to do something unusual on behalf of our business. You'll recall that Jesus encountered a blind man and on one occasion spat in the dirt and made some mud and stuck it on his eyes. This is a little gross, right? But that's what the Father told him to do.

When Moses put his hand in and it came out leprous, or he threw his staff down and it became a snake, these were prophetic acts. Sometimes there's an act of obedience that is unusual, yet God wants you to do it. I met a man who had set aside a lot of capital to start a business, yet God told him to give away 70% of it, which the man did. Later God gave him an invention that more than recouped what he gave.

Be cautioned that this isn't mumbo jumbo. This isn't, "If I do this, then God will do that" like a spiritual slot machine. We do prophetic acts (and sometimes we just recognize God's signs) at God's directing. Why would God prompt us to do the unusual? He does so because our business in the new season needs to be marked by the miraculous. You'll recall the nation of Israel: fast-forward and they get to the edge of the Promised Land and they pray a prayer that goes something like this: "Your presence needs to go with us, because if your presence isn't with us, how are they going to know that we're any different from the other nations?" We also need the presence of God upon our business in a new way to be distinguished from business as usual. The purpose of a rēStart is to get out of business-as-usual.

Now, speaking of prophetic acts, I really encourage you to find some friends who can pray for your business on your behalf. The scripture says it's better to give than to receive. Gather a friend or two and say, "Let's make an agreement: you pray for my business. You listen to God, you find a scripture, something that comes to your mind, an instruction, a question even that you can bring to bear for my business and I'll do the same for yours. I'll pray for your business, you pray for my business. I need a prophetic jolt in my business. I need to do something. I need to see God show up in such a way that people will see." In a recent podcast I asked Cobus Visagie, CEO of African Merchant Capital, how he stayed encouraged. He said he had a good group of friends and it seldom happened that all of them were down at the same time.

Yes, this is quite an unusual sequence of events. Soot out of a furnace, tossed in the air, covers the land, and, then there's a plague of boils. We don't want harm for others. We want to see God come through for good, and sometimes a restart involves a prophetic act to kick-off a different future.

PS: Don't go and do something religious. Listen to what the Spirit is telling you otherwise your "prophetic act" will just be a pathetic act.

For a long time God has been speaking to me about building the temple and showing me the scriptures about King David downloading all the instructions and resources to Solomon for building the temple. I kept asking the Lord about what this really meant, and He kept telling me to "be strong and do the work," although I didn't really know how to apply the word practically, and I still remained dazed and confused about how to start the business. When I started this class and started to get reconnected to Kingdom-minded and -focused business people and Believers, I started to see what it meant to build the temple. Coming together in this way has been like building God's temple first through fellowship and collaboration, and the spillover effects are personal business motivation and mobilization and growth. One thing I may do differently going forward is repurpose the business idea God gave me by partnering with others in the class on various projects and possible businesses. I also think I will try to be more deliberate and intentional about my use of time, and implement a plan as God's purpose and new direction becomes clear in this post-pandemic season. —Jackie

Principle # 23: Get up early to tackle giants

In Exodus, chapter nine, verse 13. The Lord says to Moses, *"Get up early in the morning. Confront Pharaoh, and say to him..."* When we're in shelter in place (SIP) or lockdown, there's quite a bit of talk about self-care and looking after yourself. Certainly there has been a fair share of distress, of mental illness, depression, and things that really, really bother people. What I want to encourage you to do as a leader is to remember, even when there's no work to go to, get up early and get on the job. The restart will require that you be alert so get enough sleep, but not too much sleep. Get to work, even when there isn't work there. Put yourself in place where there's a discipline that you're going through; intercept the enemy in his routine.

Don't let the lockdown lead to self pity or laziness. Rest, and stay busy. By now you would have seen the principle: kings rise early so giant killers need to rise early as well. You might not be able to go to a place of business, or things could be opening up by now and you can go to "work." If you are stuck at home, certainly you don't want to just be busy for the sake of being busy. One of the benefits of this whole Coronavirus situation has been that we realized that some of the activities with which we were greatly involved were unnecessary. We don't need to do every business trip. We don't have to take every coffee connection and we don't have to have every meeting. But the fact is that it's easy to get lulled into not wanting to work. Jesus says, *"My father is always working."* And he worked.

We shouldn't be afraid of work. Yes, we work from a place of rest and we need to see what God's doing in the world so we can say, "God, how do I rise early at least in my heart, in my spirit and physically? How do I rise early so that I can intercept the king, the enemy in his way?"

What are some of the things that would prevent you from getting going again? What are some of the things that would hinder you from moving forward? Sometimes it's hope deferred. Sometimes it's the fact that we don't seem to have "a future and a hope" although scripture says we do. Identify the things that would stop you getting out of bed in the morning and tackle them even if it takes an alarm clock or a strong cup of coffee to give you a jolt. Do what it takes to rise early and tackle the enemy in the midst of their routine.

Principle # 24: God always has a "so that"

There are principles that underpin the restarting of our work, our lives, or our businesses in this time of stretched-out uncertainty. The principle in this chapter is this: God always has a "so that." God always has a reason; He never acts randomly. Man is opportunistic in a crisis; God is deliberate. In Exodus 9:13 we saw God said to Moses, *"Get up early in the morning, confront Pharaoh, say to him, this is what the Lord, the God of the Hebrews says, let my people go so that they may worship me or this time I will send the full force of my plagues against you and your officials and your people so you may know that there is no one like me on all the earth."* "So that you may know." God acts to achieve a "so that."

Lots of people will be trying to get glory out of this crisis. There's a famous politician who said, "You never let a crisis go to waste." There are economists, healthcare specialists, politicians and businesspeople who are trying to be opportunistic with this crisis, but God has a "so that" for this season. While others are trying to consolidate power and control people and introduce a culture of fear and control; while governments are trying to stretch beyond their mandate; when businesses are using the crisis as an excuse to not pay people and not do what they are supposed to do, God has a purpose. Likewise, those who control money supply or control capital may try to pull more power to themselves. This is quite common in a crisis. Organizations go bankrupt, they go out of business and those with capital come in and buy up cheap assets. Many are specialists at exploiting their agenda in the crisis. God's "so that" still triumphs.

God's "so that" is so *"that you may know that there is no one like me in all the earth,"* and this needs to be our prayer during the coronavirus crisis. The racial tension that's going on, the economic woes that are already upon us... we need to determine align our "so that" with God's purpose: "that you will know that there is no one like me in all the earth." We see some people power grabbing, glory seeking, or clamoring for attention, but for God's children the "so that" is that his glory increases on the earth. Invite God into your situation with his "so that" agenda then his glory, his character, his person, his wonderful attributes, his goodness, his kindness, his power and his strength can be shown in you and through you in this exciting season.

The big takeaway is the understanding that I'm in the desert. I know the desert not supposed to be a great place, but it helped me really understand the importance of purpose and how being in Egypt, where from the worldly point of view I had everything, the top-notch company and a role that so many people would just do anything for... but it didn't feel right. And, and how important purpose is because, even understanding you're in Egypt... there's a purpose. And God's a part of it, and you see God working. And so whether I go back to a similar kind of position, or I am meant to do something different, having that underlying purpose is incredibly important, I've realized.—Anne-Marie

Principle # 25: Plagues pull down false gods

This chapter underscores the principle that God does things to achieve his purposes in history.

> *For by now I could have stretched out my hand and struck you and your people with a plague that would have wiped you off the earth. But I have raised you up for this very purpose, that I might show you my power and that my name might be proclaimed in all the earth.*

Many historians believe that the plagues were representative of the gods of Egypt. My research indicates there were many more than 10 gods that the Egyptians worshiped. You can do your own homework, but the fact is that symbolically, at least, specific gods — the gods on which Egypt had relied — were dealt a blow through the plagues. What's that got to do with us today? Well, you might rightly call the Coronavirus a plague. Certainly there are other plagues or things that bother us on the earth. The purpose of a plague is sometimes to rid us of false gods.

Many might say we believe in Jesus, we believe in the virgin birth, the resurrection and all the basic tenets of the faith so there is no way that we have any false gods. Whenever we place our reliance on something other than God, when our focus is on building a kingdom which is not the kingdom of God, have we not set up a false God? When our ambition, our leisure, our exercise, our annual holiday to Europe, our prestige in society, our role in the church preoccupies us, have we not set up an idol? When we are enamored by the fact that they call us by this title or that title, is that not a false god? When we place anything before dependence on

God, whether it is our retirement policy, investments in a balanced portfolio, our holdings of properties... when we have a reliance on things or we place a value on things above God, don't we have false gods?

Perhaps this an ideal time to say, "God, you know everything: the things I'm relying on, depending on, hoping for, aiming at, or setting my eye on. You know when I do not have you as my first priority." This is a time to reset. This is a season to say, "I want to fix my eyes on the horizon. I want to set my gaze on that which lies ahead and not just go about serving the things that are already built into my life portfolio or lifestyle."

God wanted Egypt and Israel to be rid of the false gods. In fact, he wanted Israel to be rid of the false gods in their heart. When he gave The 10 Commandments he said, "You shall have no other gods before me." Today he whispers to us, "I want you to be totally free from error, from untruth, from anything that would detract from my full purposes for you, and my full purposes for you with me in the earth." Plagues have a way of highlighting false gods. Let's take this time to reflect and to say, "God, am I dependent on anything, have I elevated anything, have I looked to, trusted in, relied on anything before you and you alone?"

Principle # 26: You cannot negotiate obedience

We are still in the Book of Exodus where Pharaoh might just be starting to buckle under pressure and is beginning to negotiate. He says, "Okay, Moses, I will let the people go, but only the men should go." In fact, he posed it as a question: "I'm going to let you go, but who exactly is going to be going?" This it's very interesting because we do the same thing in our lives. We try to negotiate a partial obedience with God. But our principle for this chapter is clear: obedience is not a negotiation. God is not actually interested in our clever negotiating strategies, and Pharaoh tried this with God. First he tried to negotiate distance, "Don't go too far, just worship here." Then he tries to negotiate who is included in the deal. "Okay, you can go, but leave the women and children behind. Don't take all your animals, et cetera." Pharaoh somehow thinks that he has a negotiating position.

I also naïvely think I have a negotiating position with God, but I don't. Obedience is all-in. Worship is all-in, because God is not interested in me keeping one foot in Egypt and one foot in the Promised Land. It doesn't work that way. "Ah God, when it comes to my Sources of Income I want the predictable income stream from the River Nile, but when it comes to Benefits I want the abundance and growth of the Promised Land."

It doesn't work that way. We have to be all-in when it comes to the Kingdom of God. Jesus says, "If you put your hand to the plow and look back, you're not worthy of the Kingdom of God." A man who used to work at Price Waterhouse like me once called and said, "Brett, there's not a week that goes by that I don't think about going back to Egypt." What's he saying? There's not a week that goes by that I don't think,

"Wasn't it nice to get a regular paycheck?" We have rosy recall of where we've come from. The Jews said this to Moses. "Why didn't you just leave us in Egypt? We'd rather be slaves there: at least we had food, at least we had a place where we could live." And while we may have overly fond memories of the past, God doesn't want to get us stuck with rose-tinted amnesia, forgetting what we should remember, and remembering what we should forget. He actually wants us completely out of the Kingdom of Darkness and into the Kingdom of Light.

Repositioning is a legal matter. God has repositioned us. We used to be enemies, now we're friends. We were slaves, now we are free. How then can we go on living as if we want to serve two masters? We want to serve a system that we should be coming out of and then also get the benefits of the system that we're going into. My brother once said to me, "Brett, Promised Land principles don't work in the Desert, and they don't work in Egypt." God wants to teach us a new set of principles. Obedience isn't a negotiation.

God has no interest in us going halfway. He wants us all-in, for his good and for our good, but particularly for us. It's most important that we realize the things that God wants us to be rid of at this time so that we can have a renewed mind, a renewed spirit, a renewed heart, and be fully free to live in the Promised Land.

Right now, we've talked a lot about getting out of the land of Egypt, and we need to understand what that looks like. As we go forward we'll be having more our focus to think about what it means to be in and to live in the Promised Land.

Principle # 27: Don't call good evil and evil good

Our next principle is particularly relevant at a time in history when society is struggling to find the truth: don't call good evil, and evil good. The enemy of your soul will do so for you.

As you purpose to go after God and follow him fully, as you intend to have a kingdom business or career, if the enemy cannot keep you from doing this out of fear he will do it using guilt. If he can't change your desire, satan will try to "guilt you" into staying where you are.

Listen to this account. Pharaoh said, *"The Lord with you. If I let you go along with your women and children, clearly you are bent on evil."* So here's Pharaoh telling Moses and team that they are bent on evil. Isn't it odd that in the midst of obnoxious behavior from Pharaoh he tries to tell Moses and Aaron that they are the bad guys. Satan does the same with us. "If you really were a good Christian, you'd never want to leave. If you're a good Christian, you would comply. If you're a good Christian, you would do something that is contrary to the word of God." It is sneaky how the enemy tries to take a moral stance to keep us from doing what God wants us to do. (We see this in society where morally bankrupt people paint themselves as righteous in order to shame Jesus followers into passivity.) Jesus encountered this in the desert where he was tempted. The scripture says, "If you are the son of God..."

The strategy of the enemy is to do anything that will keep us in Egypt, including blaming us for being the guilty party. The longer this pandemic continues the more control-oriented governments are going to want to keep their people under its spell then point a finger at those who are trying to achieve some level of freedom. They do so as an excuse to further ongoing tyranny, perhaps. It could also be that leaders who get a taste of unchecked power rarely give it up. This is symbolic of what the enemy of our souls does to us, trying to keep us enmeshed in a system from which we should be liberated.

You want to have a kingdom business—that's awesome! You want your daily work to expand the kingdom of God—this is an excellent pursuit. For this to happen, our minds need to be renewed radically. We need to see the things that have stopped us from getting ahead in terms of our kingdom endeavors, be loosed of them, and not be held back because of guilt. Some of that guilt comes from well-meaning Christians who say, "Ah, but orthodoxy suggests," or "A good Christian does this," or "...doesn't do that." Discern when it's the voice of man and the voice of God. Be careful to not get guilted into staying in a place of mediocrity, camping where we've always been. It is particularly possible that this notion of a false guilt will keep us from pursuing God with the rest of our lives. Don't get under false guilt; get free quickly. The kingdom depends on it. The future of your business depends on it.

This is even more true at the national level. Watch a political debate and each party is trying to paint their picture as righteous and the other as scandalous. This is done with clever language, of course, labeling the inhumane of immigrant children as "border security" or the murder of unborn children "freedom of choice." We who claim to know truth have become stupid when it comes to discerning good from evil. We have opted to think along party lines rather than in alignment with biblical truth. We look for answers in personalities but fail to discern spirit(s) that lie behind the platforms underpinning the parties. We should not blur clear distinctions between good and evil just because our chosen political party defines things in a particular way. "Don't call good evil, and don't call evil good" or you will get a restart, but in the wrong direction.

PS: If you are tempted to close the book and not continue because I have just offended you then you probably have greater deference to a political spirit (whether it comes with a Republican, Democrat) than the Holy Spirit. Take a deep breath, deal with it, and keep reading.

Principle # 28: Signs in nature can be supernatural

How do we know what God is doing? How do we know what He is saying? One of the things we can do is take clues from nature. Sometimes when we see things happening in nature it's a clue for us of what he's going to be doing going forward. This is definitely not always true, but sometimes... Just today I was reminded about the super-blooms in California in recent years that have preceded a new wave of revival.

Let me give you a few examples out of the book of Exodus. Exodus 10:22, *"So Moses stretched out his hands towards the sky and a total darkness covered all Egypt for three days."* Three days of dark, darkness. Here comes Jesus. Remember the three hours of darkness when Jesus died. He was in the tomb. Nature sometimes points to things that are to come.

> *And the Lord changed the wind to a very strong west wind, which caught up the locusts and carried them into the Red Sea. Not a locust was left anywhere in Egypt. Exodus 10:19*

"And the Lord changed the wind to a very strong west wind, which caught up the locusts and carried them into..." where? The Red Sea. Oh, who is the next thing that ends up in the Red Sea? Pharaoh's army!

Let's be reasonable. If God, the God of Heaven, can take locusts like they had never seen before and uproot them and put them into the Red Sea, is it too hard for him to do it with Pharaoh's army? Pharaoh should have got a clue from some of the natural events that were going on.

Sometimes we also need to get a clue from some of the things that God is doing in the natural, around us. Be attentive to what God is doing, not in some mystical or weirdo way, but with a naturally supernatural alertness of spirit. I am shocked at how many genuine followers of Jesus are not tuned into the meta narrative of what God is doing in history and are pursuing petty political or religious preferences.

It's good to read scripture, and it's good to have other "good news" sources that will feed us truth. Before we consume the daily news we have to have discernment to make sure we don't just collect a version of the truth that suits our view of the world and keeps us stuck where we are.

Watch what God is doing in multiple realms. Watch out for twisted news. We can get a clue as to what God might be doing from what we see happening in the economy. What do you see happening in terms of globalization? What do you see happening in terms of major changes in the world? Look at the trustworthiness of nations: some nations are proving to be untrustworthy.

I sat with two groups of entrepreneurs recently, and we brainstormed some of the opportunities that are coming out of this crisis. I have two full mind-maps on that topic, because we tried to understand the times. We tried to look at what's going on in the world and say, "God, is there an opportunity for greater service coming out of this crisis?" Is there something that we can explore for good as we see what's happening in the natural, in the economy, in media, in healthcare, in governments? What are the opportunities for your people? How can we see what you're doing through just some of the more natural things that we see around us?

Keep your eyes open, keep your heart open, and look for the opportunities to serve.

Principle # 29: Do not curse so you don't get cursed

I'm going to jump forward a little bit today into Exodus chapter 22 just to highlight a principle. "Do not blaspheme God or curse the ruler of your people." We all live in countries, states and cities where there are rulers of our people. The principle is this: you don't curse your way into blessing. For Pharaoh, the tip is clear: the curses you lay on God's people will come back on you. In Exodus 10:28, Pharaoh said to Moses, *"Get out of my sight. Make sure you do not appear before me again. The day you see my face, you will die."* That's a pretty heavy message.

Now I understand there is truthful news and there is fake news. People claim that their news is real news and another person's news is untrustworthy. There's a lot of information flying around. Behind the news reports and commentary there is something more sinister: a lot of cursing happens. People curse leaders, people curse people in government, people curse white people, black people, police, and so forth and so on. Yes, there are wonderful stories of praise. We praise first responders but we suspect everybody from Bill Gates to the Chinese government, to the American government, to... you name it. There is plenty of cursing going around, yet scripture says "the power of life is in the tongue." And God says He puts before us blessings and curses, and we need to look at the conditions for blessings.

One of the conditions for blessing is that we do not curse our leaders. What happened in this lesson is that Pharaoh speaks almost a curse over Moses and team and says, "Look, the next time you see my face, you're going to die." Shortly thereafter, what happens? Pharaoh's army is drowned and perhaps he drowned too. Historians don't agree whether he drowned or not, but Psalm 136 verse 15 has an inference where it says, *"You swept Pharaoh and his army into the Red Sea."*

The fact is, Pharaoh cursed Moses and Aaron and the curse that he placed on them came to rest upon himself. Proverbs 26: 2 says, *"Like a fluttering sparrow or a darting swallow, an undeserved curse does not come to rest."* In a time when a lot of people are saying a lot of things, spewing disparaging remarks all over the place, we as people need to rise up and be a people who bless and do not curse. We think it's woke. (Lance Wallnau says "woke" is a fake form of awakening.) We think it's smart to trash talk. We think it's cool to slander our leaders, whether government leaders, political leaders or other leaders. It's not. It is cursing, and we need to be people who speak blessings.

You do not curse your way into a blessing. We need to be people who carry a blessing and who speak blessing. It's not hard to do, but it takes a discipline to break the habit of being people who speak with a forked tongue. Out of one side of our mouth comes a curse and out of the other side comes a blessing.
Jesus said, *"You can't get bad fruit and good fruit off the same tree."* I remember once when we lived in South Africa, we had an orange tree, and lo and behold, shortly thereafter, it started producing lemons. I went down and one tree had been grafted onto the other and now the same tree produced bitter fruit and sweet fruit. That's a rare thing. Let's not try that for ourselves. Let's be people who speak blessing so that we live out a blessing.

Principle # 30: Our free will can keep us in Egypt

We are looking at tips for restarting and there is caution in today's principle: our free will can keep us in Egypt. There is a parallel tip for the Pharaohs of this world: eventually, you will run out of grace, you will run out of runway. Moses replied, *"Just as you say, I'll never appear before you again."* Now, Pharaoh did summons him again, but only to tell Moses to get out of the country. We can have a stubborn refusal to see what God is doing, and we can be determined to stick to the old way of doing things. Remember, this is a season in the world in which there's an opportunity for a divine reset, where there's a divine possibility for God to say, "Okay, change things up, Brett. The way you might've been doing business is not the way I want you to do it going forward."

We can get stuck in old ways of worship: where we worship, with whom we worship, how we worship. We can get stuck with false gods. We can get stuck in a flawed economic system, but Moses says to Pharaoh, "Just as you say." So, recognize that your free will can keep you in Egypt. God's not going to force us to leave. We have a responsibility to make decisions that move ourselves in the right direction. We have to ask ourselves at a gut level, whether we're enamored with, perhaps even in love with, the systems of the world, the way they work, the things that have fed us, the way they have clothed us, the benefits that have emanated from its economic model. Or are we willing to be people who will go through the desert, go through a stripping down, a rewiring so that we're equipped to live in the Promised Land?

The good news is, eventually the enemy will run out of runway, but let's not take it for granted that we are going to move to the place God wants us to move. Because if we're determined to stay in Egypt he will let us stay. How do you want to come out of this crisis? Do you want to come out differently positioned? Do you want to come out better equipped? Or have you just taken a small rest and you just want to go back to business as usual? God might be happy for you to do business as usual if that business was what he wanted you to do. He might be content for you to stay in your corporate job, your government job, your education job, because that's exactly where he has you, and he has you there on assignment. Make sure, however, that as you go forward you've taken the time to ask, "God, is this the way you want things to be? Is this the road that you're going to give me the grace to travel?"

Let's not lose this opportunity because if we don't even ask the question by default the answer is that we will stay where we are. Ask the right questions. It could determine the trajectory of your new normal.

Principle # 31: See what's trending and go with it

Scripture is replete with principles of restart and this one is particularly interesting. We need to know when the momentum has shifted and we need to go with that momentum.

In Exodus 11:3 we read that the Lord made the Egyptians favorably disposed towards the people. (It says this in brackets actually, which gives us a hint about favor: it comes as a by-product of obedience, but seldom comes when we go after it. Favor is a fruit, not a pursuit.) *"And Moses himself was highly regarded in Egypt by Pharaoh's officials and by the people."* What's happened? We have this fellow, Moses, but he's a nobody. He left Egypt 40 years after having killed an Egyptian: he went AWOL, was off the Cairo social circuit, but now comes back an 80-year-old man. Who is he? He is a nobody in Egypt and a persona non grata with the Jewish people, but as this nobody hears God, obeys, and speaks to the king, God confirms his word with signs and wonders and he becomes a somebody. The momentum shifts from the all-powerful Pharaoh to this shepherd that comes out of the desert with a serious suntan, a big beard and plenty of wrinkles. The pendulum has swung towards Moses.

Moses was born a problem because he was a Jewish boy, who became a prince, who became a problem because he murdered somebody and fled to the desert, who became a prophet called by God to speak to Pharaoh, who became a problem again because the Jews experienced difficulties as soon as Moses starts speaking to Pharaoh, and who became a prince again. If you don't persist, you won't be a prince. If you don't hang in there when there's opposition, if you don't remain with your prophetic nose at the coalface then you

91

won't get through to where the momentum shifts. So, staying in the game is part of what builds momentum. Getting back into your business, marketing again, selling again, serving customers, calling them, getting back in the saddle even when things have been difficult: this is part of what takes us from being a problem to being a prince. Persistence helps bridge us from purpose-lost to purpose-found.

The momentum in the battle between Moses's God and the Egyptian's god had shifted. Moses was trending. The key understanding is when the momentum shifts don't back off. Keep your pedal to the metal, as they say. Keep pressure on the assignment, because otherwise 'we clutch defeat from the jaws of victory.' It's as if God is about to give us a victory and we back away. When God causes you to trend don't be timid. Do not back away and say, "Oh, it's all about God." Endure the pressure in the situation—with persistent endurance—so that you can morph from being a problem to being a prince.

"So far in the course I have started to realize that the different of spheres of my life as convergence is starting to happen. I have started to become calm and begun to ask God how I can partner with him. I am somebody who's always been about me, competing, but right now I feel more and more challenged to say, "This that I do, how can it be about the Kingdom? How can I be obedient? How I can hear what is on the Father's heart?

Moving forward I am starting to question a lot about my current business model. Whether I should go on or I need to look for products that bring glory to the Father. That is what I am starting to see and I am praying that God gives me the wisdom and the power to see this to the end and to start to repurpose myself and the business. reStart has pushed me to really think about my responsibility and accountability for facing the giants. Is life all about me? Is it all about money? About being first? I believe God wants me to rebuild, revive, and restore meaningful livelihoods. I want to raise up Kingdom entrepreneurs. I want to coach and disciple."—Brian

Principle # 32: God resets your calendar

There's been a lot of talk about the new normal and what the new normal is. Do we know what it is, or are we aiming to go back to business as usual? Imagine this: Israel had been in Egypt for more then ten generations. After that amount of time one gets used to the way things are, and the land you are hoping to go to seems distant. What reignited their hope? Exodus Chapter 12:1, the Lord said to Moses and Aaron in Egypt, *"This month is to be for you the first month, the first month of your year."* The principle here is that God resets your life calendar not just your clock. He determines when life is beginning again for you. Scripture says that God is the God of new beginnings. And so, we have an opportunity to have a new beginning with God coming out of this worldwide pandemic.

The restarting of our seasons is something that is God's prerogative. God is the God of new beginnings and we endeavor to understand the season in which he has us. This gives us hope. We can go to God and say, "Father God, I need a seasonal reset. I need the beginning of a new season in my life." Most of us live with the tension caused by the fact that God has spoken to us about things and said, "You're going to live life over there," and actually we're over here. And in between, there's a gap, and that gap is a faith-gap. In other words, there's a gap between what God has said and what we've seen come to pass as yet.

This can be a problem because the enemy can exploit that God-allowed gap. For example, you believe God wants to heal everybody, but not everybody is healed and the enemy can exploit that differential. Your children grew up with you believing God is going to provide this and that but it didn't happen the way they thought and there's a gap which can be exploited. Know that living with this divine tension is part of kingdom living. We have a kingdom that's here and not here yet, and we have to live with these two worlds.

Scripture promises Jesus will return. Christ will be coming back, but we don't know when.

> *Dear friends, now we are children of God, and what we will be has not yet been made known. But we know that when Christ appears, we shall be like him, for we shall see him as he is. All who have this hope in him purify themselves, just as he is pure.* 1 John 3:2-3

"And everyone who has this hope in him purifies himself..." And so, we are people of a present season and people of a future season. Part of our desire and our operation as faith-based people is we say, "This is where we are. This is reality. This is where we want to be. This is our hope. This is our aspiration." Then we invest our prayer, our time, our faith, our obedience, our trust in God, the God of the future, the God who calls things that are not as though they are.

Faith bridges the gap between the now and the not yet. It's our faith that builds a ladder between where we are and where are we going to end up. We stand in faith knowing that God is the God who resets our seasons. Come to God, ask Him for a seasonal reset. "This will be the first month in your year." This is God's prerogative to call it out. Let Him call out a new season for you. Ask Him, "What is my season, what's my future season about?" And let Him speak that to your heart so that you can follow Him with clarity, with obedience and with hope. He is the God of all hope. *"And hope does not put us to shame, because God's love has been poured out into our hearts through the Holy Spirit, who has been given to us."* Romans 5:5 I'll meet you in the next chapter... where you may well be in a new season.

"reStart has helped me to reframe, not just my business but all areas of my life." —
Felicia

Principle # 33: The sharing economy is so BC

In recent years, there's been quite a bit of talk about the sharing economy. Can you think of some examples? Uber is one of them with its ride sharing or sharing a vehicle; Airbnb is another where you share a room or a house. Books have been written about a sharing economy. The sharing economy is not just before-Covid, it is before Christ. (BC)

In Exodus chapter 12, this is what scripture says: *"If any household is too small to eat a whole lamb, they must share one with their nearest neighbor, having taken into account the number of people there are."* The principle for this chapter is that there's no waste in a sacrifice. God is extravagant, but he told them to only sacrifice what they could eat and to share with their neighbor so that there wasn't needless slaughter of the lambs. He gave instructions that precluded waste.

Many of us are in a time when we we're waiting to get jump-started to go to the next level. We might be waiting for a capital infusion, waiting for new clients, waiting for new products to take off. We've been writing books or putting courses together or developing new products that can be delivered online instead of face-to-face. We've been thinking about new partnering situations. We've been thinking about how we shorten our supply chains so we can get closer to the customer.

As we think about these things we have surely contemplated removing some of the inefficiencies of intermediaries: we've been thinking about disintermediation. God has been ahead of us in this principle. A crisis can open our hands to share with others while we wait for a resolution. We have extra this, we share it with somebody, they have extra that, and they share it with us. There can be a delight in the sharing together of God's people as they prepare to move. There can be an efficiency, not an inefficiency, in the face of promise.

Sometimes we have baggage because we haven't shared what we have, and that baggage can hold us back. Take a look at what you have and say, "Could I be blessing somebody else with what I have right now? Do I have too much? Can I be offering things to somebody else, somebody who is going to go on the journey with me, so that they're encouraged, they're prepared?"

Jesus taught it is better to give than to receive. One of the things that I've been encouraging in the people who've been going through our rēStart course is to pray for somebody else's business, as a start, and also consider how they give referrals to other people, how they can share. The idea of a sharing economy is not new. The idea of efficiency is not new. The idea of clear process is not new. We now have a clear opportunity to say, "God, with whom can I share? Is there something which, if I don't share it, it'll hold me back? How do I bless somebody else's business, somebody else's initiative, what somebody else wants to do?"
Recently, I finished up a three-hour phone call with somebody. They'd asked for a one-hour but needed advice on a whole range of topics. At the end, they said, "I want to invest in you." Now, I don't know what they mean, but I was blessed by their sentiment, by their desire. Find somebody to invest in, with whom you can share, somebody with whom you can enjoy a meal, even if it's virtually. The Sharing Economy is not a 21st Century invention.

"It's all starting to come together and taking me literally from the desert into the Promised Land in such a short period of time."—Debbie

Principle # 34: Care for it, sacrifice it

We talked in the previous chapter about the sharing economy. I want to dig a little bit deeper. What happens, as a reminder, is God says to the Israelites, *"You are to get a lamb without defect, a male. And what you need to do is this: you must care for it for 14 days."* Exodus 12:6. Here's the principle: sometimes we need to get attached to things before we sacrifice them. Scripture goes on to say, *"Care for it for 14 days and then you slaughter it."* Now, by that stage, after 14 days, the Jewish kids probably had pet names for those little lambs. "Oh this one is so cute, we're going to call it Fluffy, we're going to call it Wooly." Back when I lived in Hout Bay in South Africa the kids in the local school caused a bit of a riot. Every year the school had a school fair which was a fundraiser. One year the principal decided to buy a small flock of lambs. What was the idea of the teachers and the principal? They wanted to let the cute lambs graze around the school grounds for a couple of months until they were nice and fat, and then they would get the local butcher to kill them and put them on the braai/BBQ. As the day of the big event approached the kids signed a petition. By now they'd given these lambs names and they had no intention of letting the mercenary teachers proceed with their plan. (I suspect they probably sold them to a butcher anyway, and just got some money.) But the fact is the kids had become attached to the lambs.

Sometimes God wants us to become attached to something before we sacrifice it. It might be your career, your work, or your business that has been a little lamb to you. For others it could be your investment portfolio, that special thing that you hold dear. You hold it close but, if you're not careful, it's going to hold you back from the move that God wants you to make. Did you know that it can be the sacrificing of your special thing that protects you for the future? Remember the blood of the lamb on the doorposts and the lintels is what prevented the angel of death from going into their houses. Sometimes when God calls us to sacrifice something which is dear to us, something that's been good to us and we've become attached to, it is so that we can move into the next season that we have in life... alive!

Sometimes we need to get attached to things before we sacrifice them. Think about what these things might be in your life and how freedom can come as things that have been good (they've been assets in the past) are left behind because God doesn't want them to go across the Red Sea into the desert. Determine what those things are, so that you can willingly offer them to God.

Principle # 35: Fat bread doesn't make for fast starts

Here is our next restart principal: Fat bread doesn't make for fast starts. Say that quickly: Fat bread doesn't make for fast starts. In Exodus 12:8 scripture says, "*That same night, they are to eat the meat roasted over the fire, along with bitter herbs and bread made without yeast.*"

We need to keep flat bread, a flat belly, and a flat wallet if we're going to be ready to move at the speed that God wants us to move. When you're traveling on an airplane, they tell you, "In the unlikely event of an emergency, move to an exit and jump onto the evacuation slide. Take off your high heels. Leave your briefcase behind. Leave your laptop behind... leave everything behind and jump out the window or door." This is a little bit what it was like when the Israelites were leaving Egypt. What seems to be tasty now can become a burden to us later. Sarah and Samuel might have been thinking, "What would go nicely with this lamb is a little bit of red wine and a nice chunk of good old Egyptian bread."

Recently we were in Cairo, which has very dusty roads, and as we drove down the street and there was a motorbike, and on the back of the motorbike was a huge basket with loaves of bread. They have a puffy bread that's crispy on the outside. Maybe some of the Israelites were tempted to take some of those puffy, fat Cairo breads with them. They might have tasted good, but there would have been a burden to them or a hindrance to them moving quickly and traveling light.

So, fat bread doesn't make for fast starts. When God says that we are to take bread without yeast He has good reason

102

for it. Sometimes there have been things that have just been awesome for us in the past. They have been great. They have worked well: products, marketing strategies, customer segments or even cities where we've done business. Then God says, "No more. I don't want that to go into your future. It's been great, but it's not what's needed to advance the kingdom in the future."

And this is the plumb line for us. Obviously, we want to do what pleases God, what blesses people and that which meets genuine needs. In addition, we should also be asking, "God, what do You want to do with me in a future season?" This will make us more prepared to pursue what He has for us.
So, take your flatbread but not your high heels: we're heading out and we just might have to go quickly, so be prepared.

Principle # 36: Restart and travel light

During this shelter in place, lockdown, stay in place, whatever it might've been for you, people developed all sorts of ways to entertain themselves. The reality is, in the case of the Israelites, God said to them, "You have this special meal that you're going to need to eat, but this is how you are to eat it." He says, *"With your cloak tucked into your belt, your sandals on your feet, and your staff in your hand."* Some of us are not ready to restart because we're still thinking about how are we going to make ourselves comfortable while we shelter in place. We're thinking about self-care, et cetera. But God says to the Israelites, "You're going to have this special meal, and you're going to have it with certain ingredients, without yeast, etc. And this is how you must be dressed." Little did they know, as there they are just having their meals, sleeping in their clothes... little did they know that it wasn't just some symbolic ritual. It was essential preparation because that very night the Angel of Death went through Egypt. In the middle of the night Pharaoh summonsed Moses and Aaron, and said, "Get out of the country." The alarm was given, they were dressed for the occasion, and they got up and left in a hurry.

It's interesting, because the scripture goes on to say in verse 34, *"So, the people took their dough before the yeast was added, and carried it on their shoulders in kneading troughs wrapped in clothing."* Picture the situation: they've been told to get ready to travel light. Now, imagine if Sarah, or Rachel, or one of these people had just snuck a bit of yeast in there. As they went through the hot desert air, what would have happened? The bread would have begun to rise, and their disobedience would have caused a burden. As they traveled with the dough wrapped in their clothing carrying their kneading troughs, if the dough had yeast in it, it would have expanded, and old Rachel would have looked like the hunchback of Notre Dame.

When God tells us, "I want you to travel light. I want you to be ready to go," we shouldn't just sneak some stuff in from our past business practices or our past business model that worked because it could become a burden to us as we go forward. Inertia is almost a guarantee that we'll stay in Egypt, and the present crisis would've been wasted on us. When we decide to tuck into our pocket, tuck into our portfolio, tuck into our product strategy, something that God says leave behind in Egypt it will become a problem for us. But as we step out in obedience, without any leaven in that bread, without any yeast in that bread, it'll cause us to be mobile, to be fleet-footed, and to be ready for that which lies ahead. So, restart and travel fast.

Principle # 37: Bloody business protection

The question in this chapter might seem strange: is there blood on your business? Scripture says, "When I see the blood, when I see the blood..." It was talking, of course, about the blood of the sacrificed lamb on the lintel and the doorpost of the Jewish people. It was referring forward, as we know, to the blood of Jesus on our lives and that when that is present then the angel of death doesn't come into our house. Now, some people do not want an association with Jesus in their business. My work life is over here--my spiritual life is over there. I don't want to mix church and business. I don't want to mix God and business.

A good friend of mine said, "You can separate church and state, but you cannot separate God and government." Scripture says, "Of the increase of His government and peace, there will be no end." When you kick God out of a business or you kick God out of a government, there's not a vacuum that remains: that vacuum is filled by some other god, some other philosophy. This seems to be what has happened in America. From where I'm sitting at the moment, we have spent decades trying to whitewash the public space and get God out of business, get God out of schools, out of government. And in many respects, we are reaping the consequences, not of a godless society where there's just a vacuum... No, that vacuum has been filled by the philosophies of men. Humanism and political correctness, among other "-isms" have rushed into the vacuum that has been left by us telling God to step out of our public life. The covering has been damaged.

Nowadays everything has to be labeled as business, economics or science. There's no sign of the blood. When reporters are commenting on news, they say, "Well, this is science. This is economics. This is business." Not, "God, we need your help. We need a national day of prayer. We need your intervention." Yes, we might say at the end of an event, "God bless America," but actually we've asked God to stay out of America. We've asked God to stay out of the running of our countries and our economies. Is there blood on our nations? Is God seeing the blood of King Jesus on our work and businesses?

We've talked a bit about the question God once asked me, "When is a business dead?" and we know a business isn't dead until God says it's dead. But sometimes we invite the kiss of death because we've kicked the King of Kings out of our day-to-day business life. Surely, this shouldn't be. Sometimes the concept of blood on a business sounds like a terrible thing. In this case, it's a good thing. Commit your business to God. Invite Jesus to be the CEO. Commit to doing business not just with godly principles, but for a godly purpose. Don't try to separate God and business or work and faith: they were made to be integrated. You can separate church and state, but you cannot separate God and government. You can separate, if you like, the church as an institution owning businesses, but you can never separate faith in work. Keep the blood on the business.

Principle # 38: Feed faith, starve fear

The principles we are exploring in this book are rocks in your foundation which, when taken together, will help you set a base for restarting your business. The opportunity is not to just have the same old business as it was in the past, but to have it reset for what God wants to do in the future. The principle we're digging into today comes from Exodus 12:23, *"And He will not permit the destroyer to enter your houses and strike you down."* God draws circles around the destroyer. You can say to God as you look at your business, "God, this is a business that you started. This business started because you spoke a word to me and I responded in faith. This business began decades ago, years ago." And you can feed on faith and starve fear. You can remind Him, "Father, this is yours, and since you initiated it, you need to preserve it. You need to put a circle around it so that the destroyer does not come near it."

Jesus asked, *"Why do you fear people who can destroy your body, but you don't fear God who can destroy your soul?"* If God can preserve our soul, He can preserve our business. How do we protect our business in time of crisis? We stand in faith and we draw a circle around it in prayer. We plead the covering of the blood of Jesus over it. And we say, "God, this is your business for your purpose. What glory is there in this business going down to the corporate tomb?" Now, I'm not saying that there shouldn't be aspects of my business or your business that shouldn't be pruned. Yes, God prunes the fruitful areas for greater fruitfulness. He cuts off the unproductive areas. We can emerge leaner and more focused, but we shouldn't fear death. We shouldn't fear, "what if?" What if this thing is just going to die? We have to say, "This is God's. I've given it to him. And so, I am going to stand in faith that God will preserve this business."

Recently, there was a company in Cape Town and they were in serious difficulty. And the banks, the accountants, the lawyers said, "You're bankrupt. You need to shut down the business." One of my colleagues, Errol, said to them, "Remember the question, 'When is a business dead?'" Errol reminded them that the answer is, "A business isn't dead until I say it's dead." And with that reminder, they sought the Lord. God gave them a scripture about speaking to the dry bones, and they stood in faith on behalf of their business. They pleaded the covering of the blood of Jesus over their business. They spoke the life of Jesus into their business. Shortly thereafter they received a couple of big orders and this has since opened up a lot of things for them. The business is thriving again. You can read Hannes and Anra Visser's story between chapters 20 and 21.

Don't give up if God hasn't said your workplace or business is dead. Make sure that you plant a prayer hedge around your business and live in faith and live with hope. For some of you, you've even had to close your business, but do not live with hope deferred but with faith that something better will open on the other side for you.

Principle # 39: Sometimes deliverance comes when it is darkest

Some people are experiencing this time as a dark season. Loneliness, uncertainty and economic challenges have been rife. Mental and emotional health issues, even suicide, has become prevalent. Our principle in this chapter is therefore crucial: sometimes your deliverance comes when it's darkest. In Exodus 12:31, during the night, Pharaoh summoned Moses and Aaron. It happened at midnight, during the night. We don't know that it was exactly midnight, but there's the phrase, the concept that when things are darkest, God often shows up with a deliverance. In Exodus 12:31, Pharaoh summons Moses and Aaron. And he says, *"Up, leave my people, you and the Israelites go worship the Lord as you've requested. Take your flocks and your herds..."* Everything that Moses had asked for, they tell him to go and then Pharaoh adds, *"And also bless me."* Not only did they leave at the urging of the Egyptians, they left with plunder from the Egyptians.

Restart is not just like a two-week vacation... and then everything goes back to normal. We sometimes have to get to a darkness of soul before deliverance comes. We sometimes have to wrestle it through in the middle of the night before a fresh inkling comes as to what God wants to do with our business.

Now, I'm not wishing gloom and doom on us, but I am saying that a reset and a restart is a deep work. It's not just a few days off from work where we say, "Ah, I'll take a couple of days away from things." When God is doing a reset it's not just because there happens to be a pandemic, but he's using this to get the attention of the world. When He gets our attention it's a deep thing, it's not a surface thing. The goal isn't to see how many puzzles we can do while we're off work, or how many books we can read, or how many new hobbies we can have. No, the goal is to say, as God's people, "God, You are doing something big. You are doing something important."

This is going to be a historical marker where there's a "before corona", and there's an "after corona," not to glorify a disease. Just as there was with September 11th, or the second World War, or the assassination of certain world leaders, or people landing on the moon, there are some pivot points in history. What is happening in 2020 is one such season. Often, as we are wondering what's going to come next, deliverance comes when it's darkest. Don't give up at one minute before midnight because you don't know when your deliverance is coming. You don't know when your Pharaoh is going to summons you and say, "Up out of my land. Take your animals, your wife, your children. Take our gold, take our silver, take our artifacts, take whatever you like, but get out of my country. Go and worship your God." You don't know when that time is coming. So, be ready and don't give up when it's dark.

Principle # 40: Stay ready to travel

Pack on purpose. We find ourselves back in Exodus, chapter 12. During the night Pharaoh summoned Moses and Aaron and said, "Up, leave my people, you and the Israelites go worship." What if you are sitting back in the Jewish camp, in the Israeli quarters, and you haven't packed? You've said, "Ah, Moses told us to eat the meal and get ready to travel, but I decided I would pack in the morning." When they ate that meal, they didn't know that they'd be leaving in the middle of the night. God wants us to have a high level of readiness in this season.

Sometimes in scripture you'll see God warning someone in advance. Joseph was warned in a dream that he needed to take Mary and the child and get out of town, so he did this and fled to Egypt. At other times we'll hear Jesus telling the story of the five foolish virgins, it's typically called. (Nowadays it might be the five foolish Millennials who didn't have spare cell phone batteries. It's actually probably the old people that didn't have the spare cell phone chargers.) The bottoms line is we need to be ready to move.

I hear people saying they want to do what God wants them to do, but they don't have a passport. God's given us a commandment to go to the nations. If God gives you a commandment to go the nations and you're serious about following him, make sure you have the necessary travel documents. Make sure they're current. Be ready to travel. You can't say, "But I'll pack in the morning. I first have to go to the store and buy a few more things. I wasn't prepared." Some people during this time of the coronavirus crisis are spending time perfecting their recipes, doing puzzles, learning how to do watercolors (nothing against art)...

whatever they're doing as coping mechanisms instead of preparing themselves for the journey that's ahead. Many are investing in new skills; a high percentage of YouTube usage is educational.

Now, I'm not saying that self care isn't important and you shouldn't do some things for the sake of your own sanity. I did some watercolors myself this last week. I haven't done any puzzles, but I'll tell you it does puzzle me that people are not readying themselves for what's lying ahead.

New business opportunities: for sure there are new opportunities to serve. Supply chains are going to change. Our view of education is going to change. The role of the school versus the parent is going to change. That creates a business opportunity. Service industries that are closer to home are going to be more valued. Globalization is going to be more suspect. There are going to be opportunities for us to create services closer to home. At the same time, people are getting used to going online and consuming certain information or digitally based content online. There's a new opportunity there as well.

Get ready to travel. Don't get stuck where you are and say, "I parked my car, my business, in the garage. And when this crisis is over, I'll just roll it out and go back to normal." Use this time to make sure that you get your vehicle serviced and you get rid of anything that's superfluous to you. Be ready to travel, be ready to let your own business go as we may step into a new season. Pack for a purpose not for a picnic.

Principle # 41: Your enemies might send you out

Here we are with lesson number 41, and it is this: Sometimes your enemies will send you out. This freaks out some Christians because they think, "Ah, if my enemy is telling me to do this, then maybe that's not God. Maybe it's a trick." But what happened in this passage when Pharaoh called Moses and Aaron and said, "Get up. Get out of here," the other Egyptians came to them as well and they urged the Israelites to leave. They said, "Please leave Egypt. We've had enough of you guys. If you don't leave, we're all going to die because the angel of death had just passed through."

The principle here is to not just look to your circumstances and say, "Well, if the Egyptians are pushing me out, then maybe I should stay." No. Listen to the voice of God. The overriding factor is what has God said to you about your business? What has he said to you about your calling? What has he spoken to you about your purpose? This trumps any commentary from your enemies who might be pushing you out. Sometimes it'll be somebody who doesn't know Jesus, who actually pushes you in a direction you should go. We can take leadership from direction from pagan kings sometimes, but the overriding factor is the voice of God, how God is speaking to us.

We must therefore be tuned into the whisper of God. What has God spoken to you regarding your business? If you haven't done this, I would urge you to take the time to give God a blank sheet of paper, if you like. Just to sit down and to say, "God, what's on your heart for my business?" I remember years ago, I was reading 1 Thessalonians chapter one, and Paul says to them, to Thessalonica, a working community, "I remember you when I pray for you: Your work produced by faith, your labor of love and your endurance of hope."

Three things. When Paul says your "work produced by faith" he's talking about work, your everyday work and your labor of love. The motivation for going to work everyday is a love for Jesus, and if you love Jesus, then you have to ask, "What's on his heart?"

This is a good time to stop and to say, "Jesus, what is on your heart for my business? What would you do if this was your business? You see what I have in my hands. You see my assets, my liabilities, my skills, my passions. You see the things that I've given up on, that I don't even have hope for anymore, and you see the things that there is still a glimmer of hope, an ember which could be fan into flame. What would you do if this was your business? How would you use it? How could it serve the world?" And don't worry too much about whether the circumstances are closing your business, the government is doing this, and the tax man is doing that. The key thing is what is on God's heart for your business? You ask Him, and I'm sure He will show you. So take a moment, pause, ask God what's on His heart for your business.

> Now the children of Israel had done according to the word of Moses, and they had asked from the Egyptians articles of silver, articles of gold, and clothing. And the LORD had given the people favor in the sight of the Egyptians, so that they granted them what they requested. Thus they plundered the Egyptians.
> Exodus 12:35-36

Principle # 42: Figure out assets to take with you

I want to talk a little bit about another principle, and it has to do with both assets and liabilities. You could say it this way: Don't add your yeast on the wrong side of the Red Sea. I spoke in earlier chapters about the fact that the Jews left Egypt and they carried with them the dough and the kneading bowls, the dough without the yeast added. Why was this important? Because if they had added the yeast, then it would have puffed up, and that which looked tasty would have become a burden.

I want us to probe our personal and business balance sheets: this is an opportunity for us to evaluate our liabilities and our assets. I've worked with people going through a change in season, and I recommend that they go through their assets, look at The 10-P Model®, for example, your purpose, products, positioning, presence, partnering, and so on. Look at your assets and say, "I know this was an asset in a past season, but will it be an asset I should take forward into the next season? This was an asset for me in Egypt. Will it become a liability for me in the desert or in the Promised Land?"

You have to look at your own circumstances. Part of the question is, what do you want your future to look like? What does God want to do with this reset, this restart of your work and business? There are things that were a definite asset in some businesses. For example, if you were in retail and you had a retail store or maybe many retail stores, and now people are no longer coming to those stores, that which was an asset becomes a liability. You could also have had an online business and people weren't buying from you. Now they're buying more from you online. Online is an asset which becomes an enhanced asset.

I'd encourage us to go through and to look at our assets and liabilities afresh and ask ourselves whether the things to which we are so endeared, are they essential to or inconsequential to our future? How do we take the things and evaluate to see what should we take forward with us, and what should we leave behind? That's the question. So, stay slim, keep mobile, but more important, don't let certain things that were a positive for you become a negative in the future.

You can shelter in place. You can be on lockdown. You can gradually ease in, but make sure that as you get up, you're ready to go, you're ready to move. As you take your business to the next level, that you only take with you the things that are useful to you. God didn't say to the Israelites, "Leave everything in Egypt." He said, "Take their gold, take their silver," but they couldn't take everything with them. They had to be selective. You can only take selected things into your future, so reevaluate your assets and liabilities. Put them before God. Sit down with a friend, talk it through and say, "Okay, those were assets before, but will they be liabilities or assets going forward?"

PS: I must add a postscript to this chapter. We recently moved from one State in the USA to another and our household and office items had been in storage for about six years. Unpacking old things causes all sorts of emotions. Our business was started nearly 25 years ago and I amassed many half-finished items and there were reminders all around me of products or services that didn't reach their full potential. One day I had an epiphany. I could either try to fit this into a jigsaw puzzle of the future or I could view them as fuel that propels me to the next level. I can either waste energy trying to craft a cohesive narrative as I force-fit items into a future reality, or I can view them as an energy-giving propellant into my next season. I have chosen to do the latter. I have no desire to be one of those old guys who is dusting off his work trophies on a train that has run out of coal. Burn the trophies—they might just get you to the next source of fuel.

"The material is extremely ordered. It's order and faith. Now I can trust God for my product, my purpose, positioning and presence." —
Andries

Principle # 43: Keep your hands free for capital

Let's pick up on this theme about what you take with you into the future. The principle is simple in concept, hard in practice: Don't let temporary things fill your hands, so that you cannot carry capital. I hinted at this last time. Temporary things would be vegetables, leeks, onions, garlic, bread with yeast and perhaps even those walk like an Egyptian outfits. Permanent things would be gold, silver, jewelry, things that would create a capital base for you as you go forward.

If your hands are filled with delicacies of the Nile you won't have the space to carry real assets out of Egypt. At this time, we need discernment to figure out what is nice to have and what is going to build our capital base going forward. Keep your eye on capital preservation. There's a book out there called *Money Won't Make You Rich* by Sunday Adelaja who, at the time, was pastor, of one of the largest churches in Eastern Europe, in the Ukraine. When last I checked, which was 10 years ago, that church had 25,000 people. When the church had grown to about 15,000 people, God said words to this effect to him, "You are worse than the unprofitable servant." He said, "What do you mean God? I'm pastoring a church with 15,000 people." He said, "Yes, but you live from hand to mouth. Offerings come in and they're consumed. They're used. You're not actually building any capital. At least the unprofitable servant, the guy who had the one talent and buried it, at least he preserved the capital."

This is a principle for us as we're going through rēStart. Watch out for the preservation of capital. Many will say cashflow is king and there is an element of truth in this. It's important to stay liquid and to actually have cashflow. That said, I'm not advocating, as I saw proposed in an article written by a Christian, "Cashflow is king, so cut your payroll. Get rid of your people." No, sometimes you as the leader have to stand in faith on behalf of your people. Sometimes you need to take the first pay cut. This is what servant leadership is about. It's not what the business books teach, but we also have to figure out how we can build capital, not just cashflow. This is an important lesson for coming out of Egypt.

I have another book called 10 Steps to Restoration, which I'll release at some point in the near future. (I wrote it in 2016 but felt it was not yet time to release it.) One of the first steps in the process of bounce-back has to do with the restoration of capital. Make sure that you understand the difference between capital and working capital. If you need more on this, you can either read 2 Corinthians 9 or you can read my book 50 Principles of Faith Based Financing where you can understand these principles.

This is an opportunity, a reset time, a restart time. It's a time to reevaluate capital and say which capital, intellectual, social, relational, spiritual, and of course financial capital, do I need to preserve to take forward into the future?

I liked the Purpose session in terms of just owning what a lot of people tell me is a gift, but I've almost hesitated to really embrace it, and that's, the sense of order that I have, and putting order on chaos. Now I am actually going to lean more into that gift as a result of this course.

Also, I really liked the Assets: we're standing on your shoulders here in terms of over a decade—probably more than a decade—of your thinking. And that's been captured as knowledge management. We call it explicit versus tacit knowledge. So a lot of us as believers have tacit knowledge connecting with one another, but there's also the explicit knowledge that's been undocumented. —JP

Principle # 44: Your restart paves the way for others

Your exit from Egypt paves the way for others. My friend Fady Eldeiry is from Egypt, born in the ancient city of Alexandria. Fady now lives in the United States. He has pointed out to me that the Jews weren't the only ones who were slaves in Egypt; much of the population was in slavery. It was just the ruling class that were not slaves. In fact, there's an interesting scripture in Exodus 12:38: *"Many other people went up with them as well as large droves of livestock."* Another translation says, "A mixed multitude also went up with them."

When you leave Egypt, you create a path for others to leave with you. It is so important that we think through how we go into a brand-new way of doing business. When I say "leave Egypt" I'm not talking about the physical country, but I'm talking about leaving the economic models, the ways of doing things, and "best practices" that were present at the time but built on a wrong foundation.

It's not just good enough for Christians to do business ethically, pay their taxes, and be nice neighbors. We have to figure out how we do business God's way. This isn't just having a good intent or a good use of the bottom line by giving to charity. It means that every facet of our business needs to be sliced through and examined in light of the principles of the word of God. How do we do product development? How do we do marketing? How do we do sales? Are we using cheap techniques? Are we using principles of efficiency and best practices that are contrary to the word God? We have to examine each of these things.

We free ourselves up from those things, and we move to a better way, beyond best practices, something beyond what is offered in the world. This is true whether you're doing investing, lending money, developing products or doing mining. (Surely God had in his heart that ethical, responsible, environmentally safe mining could be done, since he placed gold, for example, in the earth, as we read about in Genesis chapter 2.)

Let's be clear that navigating your crisis doesn't give you permission to exclude so-called outsiders. The widows, the orphans, the aliens, the foreigners... God made provision for them in the new nation of Israel. Many Egyptians went with them. So just remember that as you transition from one thing to the other, take people with you. Just as Noah built an Ark for the salvation of his house, say, "God, expand the size of my boat, expand the size of my ark, so that I can take many people with me, so that others can move into the new freedom, the new purposes, the new ways of doing business that I'm experiencing with you." Remember, your exit paves the way for other people to exit as well.

Principle # 45: God resets your clock

As you have read this book you will have surmised that one of our broad themes is "Let my business go." When should a business be let go? The principle for this particular week is: "on that very day."

Now, imagine that you've been living in Egypt. You've been praying for release. "Get us out of here, get us out of this country." Things have been hard. Sometimes they've gone from bad to worse and you wonder why God isn't answering your prayer. The truth is, God's timing is bigger than our timing. It says in the Book of Exodus that *"at the end of 430 years, to the very day, all the Lord's divisions left Egypt."* 430 years to the very day, not a day too soon, not a day too late. So, God has a timing for what He's doing in history and it's bigger than your timing or my timing.

We therefore have to get in line with what He's doing otherwise we can become disappointed. On the one hand, we want to be at peace with what God is doing and content to wait for him to initiate. On the other hand, we want to make sure that we're not falling behind what God is doing. This is why we try to get an understanding of the season you are in. As I write this in 2020 during the coronavirus pandemic this is a season of restart. It's important that when God says to you, "Get up and move," that you get up and go.

What would hold us back? Fear is one thing. Another is failing to understand God's timing. Another is laziness, we just become comfortable with sheltering in place. The other is, is that we lose the habit of work. "Six days, you shall labor," says the scripture, and we've lost some that as we've been in lockdown. I read an article recently from McKinsey which urged leaders to plan for 2021 based on 2019 since the recovery is already well underway and 2020 will not be a good baseline. Unfurl your sails before the breeze is visible to the naked eye.

The other thing that's important in this passage is that the Israelites came out of Egypt "by their divisions." Jacob and son went into Egypt as a family; they came out as a nation by their divisions. And I'm hoping that we, as followers of Jesus Christ would come out of this crisis by our divisions. I don't mean more divided: I mean moving in sync as a united army, as a people who are willing to tackle the challenges in the world, willing to proceed towards the opportunities, willing to blow through obstacles like the Red Sea and lack of food and lack of water, or being attacked by various enemy forces. Because we see the Promised Land ahead of us, we need to be a people who leave because of the promise, not because of trying to just get out of pressure.

So, I encourage you, keep the promise ahead of you and understand that God is God, and we are not. He holds our times in His hands and He will say to you, "Get up and go," on that very day. 430 years to the day, He moves an entire nation. If He can move a nation on the very day, He can move your business at the right time.

I heard such great things about this [class],
but I also had the little bit of a niggling
feeling... I've done discipleship courses. I've
done a lot of leadership courses. I'm in
another leadership course right now. And I
just would say, I was so happily blown away
by how much you don't know what you don't
know. Not to say that, I think I know
everything in the least, but you just opened a
door into looking at business from God's
perspective that I haven't heard in many
different scenarios. I haven't heard anyone
presented the way that you do, ...with the
business sense with, with such wisdom, but
in humility, which is such a beautiful cycle of
just demonstrating grace.—Beth

Principle # 46: The fear of death keeps us focused

Our next principle to consider is that sometimes we need the fear of death to get us focused. God says to the nation of Israel, "Look, you need to take the blood, apply it to the lintels so that the Angel of Death passes over. And if you don't do it, your firstborn is going to die. It's going to be a problem." That ought to put the fear of God into Jewish parents, and the fear of death sometimes brings a certain amount of focus. I've actually met people who've died and gone to heaven and come back again, and it brought an urgency to their lives. People with near death experiences, they also get focused. How about your business? How about your career? As we go through, for some of us, a near-death experience it causes us to say, "What's important? What are my priorities? What is my business all about?" Is it just about building up a pension or padding a retirement package? Is it about comfortably providing for my family? Is it about giving me status? I was the director of this, the CEO of that.

Friends, death has a way of stripping from us that which is superfluous. What is superfluous in your business? What is really not that important? One of the good things the crisis has done, the current pandemic, is caused people to ask, "What is really important to me? Who are the people that I miss, who are the people I want to spend time with?" Then from a business perspective, which of my activities are really, really critical? Which products are going to bear eternal fruit, fruit that will last? Which of the activities that I engage in will produce a return, not just for my time on earth, but for eternity? Death has a way of getting us to focus.

I have to express some caution that the world will pressure you to go back to business as usual, to forget that 2020 experience ever happened. The message can be to just pump up the economy, get going, go back to normal, do business as usual... but is that what you want? Do you want business as usual or would you like your work to have more meaning? Would you like to be able to work for more than just money? Would you like to have purpose so that when you go to work every day, there's something that's a burning passion, that goes beyond just going through the motions? Have you looked at where you've been in the past and said, "Wow, that was a whole lot of activity, but I'm not sure that it added value to God's business portfolio. I'm not sure that it is producing an eternal return."

Death has a way of getting us focused. Leverage the advantages of the season.

Principle # 47: Don't escape from, consecrate to

Today we are going to dig into a principle that says we don't just escape from, we consecrate too. Let me unpack that for us a little. In Exodus chapter 13:1, the Lord said to Moses, *"Consecrate to me every firstborn male. The first of your offspring, consecrate this to me."* The key thing about getting out of Egypt or getting out of a past way of doing business is that we don't just escape from something, we actually move into something. Since a kingdom business is one which is a consecrated business where one has said, "I spend most of my working day at work; most of my time in my week is at my desk. Of the 168 hours in the week, a lot of them are spent working; this is the major portion of my waking hours. Work is therefore something that I need to give to God; it's not something that I just do and then I give God the leftovers."

A kingdom business is a consecrated business. Getting out of Egypt, restarting our business, isn't just an escape from hell, it's an entry into kingdom living. We appreciate this at the personal level and say to people, "Don't just come to Jesus to get a ticket to heaven or to get a Get out of Jail Free pass." We say, "No, no, no. The kingdom of God is now. Kingdom living and eternal life begins now." If this is true at the personal level, which it is, surely it's true at the corporate level.

What is a company? A company is a gathering of people who work together for a common purpose. In fact, the word company comes from two Italian words, *com* and *pan*, one meaning of which is "those who gather around bread." In your business, as you gather around bread, you can be a consecrated people, not just an escaping people. You have no doubt heard the occasional news flash or alert: Such and such has escaped from the XYZ prison, and they're armed and dangerous. We don't want to just be a people that escaped: we want to be a people that were led, were empowered and armed spiritually for God's purposes.

If you don't fix your eyes on the promise, you will long to go back to the good old days. This is what happened with Israel. They got into the desert and they grumbled, "Oi vey, can't we go back to Egypt already?" Why? Because they didn't have their eye on the promise. Ecclesiastes 7:10 says, *"Don't always be asking where are the good old days? Why is folks don't ask questions like that,"* it says in The Message translation. So, remember to keep an eye on the Promised Land, and develop a clear vision for the kind of business you want to have in the future. You're not just an escapee, you're somebody who's consecrated to God and to his purposes.

I just want to say this class has been phenomenal and so unexpected. Joe Gonzales prophesied over me one night and the very next morning I was in your class. He said, "Malika, I'm going to sponsor you because you've got three businesses and I want you to go to a kingdom class." Joe Gonzalez is a huge mentor in my life and just a wonderful person. I had no idea that I was going to get so much imparted to me from this class. I'm going to totally change how we expand and how we do business.—Malika

Principle # 48: Look confused, bait your enemy

We are nearly at the end of our 50 principles. You might hope to be knocking on the door of the Promised Land not still skirting the deserts of Egypt. You might have seen the tee shirt that reads "Don't follow me, I'm lost." Well, here's a principal: Sometimes, you might need to look confused to confuse your enemy. What do I mean by that? In the book of Exodus, chapter 14, they'd got out of Egypt and were heading towards the desert. And then God tells them, "Cut back, and go back towards Cairo, if you like. Go back towards where you've come from." Because the people are going to say, "These guys can't get out of the desert. They don't know how to get out of here. They're confused. They're wandering around. Let's go after them and attack them." Wow! That's a little scary if you're an Israelite, and you're hoping to get out of town and put as much distance between yourself and Pharaoh's armies as you can. And God said, "No, loop back, dangle some bait, because then they're going to pursue you." That's a little bit scary.

Sometimes God uses the foolish things to confound the wise, the scripture says in Corinthians. Sometimes your business strategies are going to look stupid to your competitors, but it's part of God's strategy to confuse the enemy. Sometimes, God may tell you to do something counter intuitive. Obey anyway. I remember once in Cape Town, I was meeting with a businessman and he had set aside R100,000 to set up a new business. Shortly thereafter he sensed God telling him to give away R70,000. That's 70% of his startup capital—not logical, to say the least. It looked stupid, but he did it. Why would God ask somebody to do that?

Well, sometimes because we're placing our trust in that capital. Sometimes, it's to test the obedience. Sometimes, it's to meet a need. That's God's business to know. Our client felt God told him to do it, and he obeyed. Shortly thereafter, he woke up in the middle of the night and he had an idea about creating a new device. I won't go into all the details but suffice is to say that he sketched it out, made a prototype, and then went to a potential customer and said, "Could you use something like this?" It was a bit of an obscure product. And the customer said, "We've been looking for something like this for five years," and placed an initial order of 32,000 units. Needless to say, he got his startup capital back.

Sometimes, God will ask you to do something that looks foolish in order to confuse your enemies, particularly, in the area of generosity, of sacrifice, and in the area of career moves. Some of you reading this have made what we could reasonably call downwardly mobile career moves or suicide job decisions. But God spoke, and if you hadn't obeyed, you wouldn't have been positioned to get a breakthrough. Yes, Israel ended up with the Egyptian army on their tail and we'll cover that in a future chapter.

For the moment, however, when God tells you to do something and it even looks a little bit stupid, if it's his revelation it is better than your calculation. Obedience is more important than logic.

A rēStart story: Debbie Jordan

Breezway Thrifty
(October 13, 2020, Southern California)

I had been struggling for four years with health issues and lost passion for day to day business when I got involved with rēp. I developed new community and made friends around the world but continued to suffer lots of depression amidst ongoing health challenges.

In 2020 I signed up for the rēStart Class with Brett, and while I still did not have clear direction I felt better. I remarked at the time, "It's all starting to come together and taking me literally from the desert into the Promised Land in such a short period of time." I was more confident about focusing on God and surrendering while I waited for the way forward to become clear.

God often speaks to me in my truck, and I was on my way to Arizona to see my daughter and new grandson, about a 5 ½ hour drive, talking to God, and heard Him tell me to sell my homes. I just recently purchased both homes so this was quite an interesting instruction. While I struggled with the decision I requested huge prayer I got lots of confirmation to move forward. I also received lots of instruction and council, including advice to change realtors. While I didn't understand everything, I did move forward. (At the same time I was re-listening to the 3-minute podcasts and was urged to obey when God speaks.) I had no idea where I would be going when the houses sold and this was stressful as I have my daughter and 3 grandchildren living with me. At some point I had to surrender and trust that every detail would work out, that this was the shift I knew was coming.

While looking for a house with a pool in a specific area a 4-acre ranch came up on the housing listings. It is perfectly laid out for my business and my home and has lots of extras for future growth. As of right now I have put my homes on the market and will be approving offers this evening on at least one house for more than I asked for. As soon as I have signed the sale contracts I am putting an offer on the ranch. Interestingly, since the first time I looked at the ranch the price has dropped $100,000.00. I am hoping for another hundred thousand. We will see. God has assured me I am fine and His plan is all that matters.

My personal assistant reminded me that this ranch in its current state with no modifications is everything I have talked about for the last 6 years. We will put the offer together for the ranch tonight and present it to the sellers this week. I meet with the zoning department in the morning to confirm I can have the business on there.

PS: Financing came through. I am approved personally for a ridiculous loan, against many odds. The change in realtors drove the prices on my house up $30,000 above what the other realtors were willing to list for. The whole thing has been crazy... and I am at peace.

Principle # 49: The fight is beyond your capability

I'm excited as we come towards the end of this restart book. Our second to last principle is quite simple: The fight is beyond your capability. The challenge you have in front of you is bigger than you can manage, and that's okay. Let's look at what happened in our Exodus story. Israel went out armed and with the beginnings of an army, but it was not enough, so they reasonably expected to die in the desert at the hands of the Egyptian army. God had told them to do this maneuver backwards towards Egypt, and now the Egyptians were on their heels. In Exodus 14, verses 13 and 14, Moses answered the people and said, *"Do not be afraid. Stand firm, and you will see the deliverance the Lord will bring you today."* The same is true for your business. Do not be afraid. Stand firm, and you will see the deliverance that God will bring you today. *"The Egyptians you see today, you will never see again. The Lord will fight for you. You need only to be still."*

Some of us have got in a panic about our businesses. Some of us have been perplexed and still God says, "Stand firm. You need only be still." This is Moses speaking bold words to the people. After he said this to the people Moses, in a move that is not uncommon among leaders, goes and he cries out to God. He was bold in front of the people, and terrified before God. God pretty much tells praying Moses, "Look, don't hold a prayer meeting. Keep moving." God says, *"Why are you crying out to me? Tell them to move on."* When God tells you to move your business, don't stop and have a prayer meeting. Don't stop and ask for another prophetic word. Don't stop and say, "God, could you reconfirm your guidance?"

Often it is more important to keep the momentum than to have a religious gathering. Movement is key. As God gets you going, keep going trusting that He will open things up for you and deal with your enemies behind you. Yes, it's okay for leaders to be bold in front of their people and meek before God, but make sure that you call your people to the right kind of action. When you need a day of prayer, have a day of prayer, but when you need to keep moving, then keep moving.

The second principle here is that sometimes God eggs your enemy on so that He can destroy them. There may have been things that have come against you, things that have been after your business, things that would seek to constrain your supply, to limit your creativity, to prevent you from being a wealth creator, or prevent you from living out your kingdom mandate. There have been things spoken against you, or there might have been things that have undermined your foundation. You've had bad partnerships, you've done the wrong kind of business deals, and these things have been sent to constrain you. They have become a trap, and a snare... yet sometimes God wants to egg your enemies on so that He can destroy them. Don't panic every time there's a bit of opposition. Say, "God, you must have a deliverance ready for me, and I'm looking forward to that deliverance."

Principle # 50: What's good for you can be bad for your enemies

You have arrived at the last of 50 principles for restarting your business we will cover in this book. (There are more in scripture, of course.) The Israelites are on their way home, but still in a difficult place as Pharaoh and his army was still in hot pursuit. Exodus 14:19, *"Then the angel of God who'd been traveling in front of Israel's army,"* (notice Israel had an army) *"withdrew and went behind them. The pillar of cloud also moved from in front and stood behind them. Coming between the armies of Egypt and Israel throughout the night, the cloud brought darkness to the one side and light to the other side."*

When God works on your behalf, when God moves us to restart our business, that which is bad for our enemies is good for us. We've seen a lot of things go wrong with the crisis, but they can be good for you. This is particularly true as regards the presence of God in your business. We must become convinced that the presence of God is what differentiates us. It's what makes the difference to our products, to our partnering, to our people, to our processes... to everything. That presence of God is what changes things.

Many have been through a season of sheltering in place. Hopefully it's taught us that we need to shelter in the shadow of the Almighty and take our company, our business, under the wings of the Almighty as we go forward. We're a people who carry a mobile tent. Some years ago, God challenged me and said, "Carry a mobile tent of meeting with you so that wherever you go you set up tent." If you're staying in somebody's house, set up tent; if you're staying in a hotel, set up tent, because the angel of God camps with us.

So, in this case, God's presence caused darkness on the one side, the cloud, the pillar of fire, the angel of the Lord, it was bad for the enemy, but it was good for Israel.

It's quite a challenging thing when things are going wrong in the world to say, "Oh God, bless me." I don't want to just pray for blessing. I don't want to talk about the blessing and the favor of God when so much is going wrong in the world. In John 10:10, Jesus says, *"The thief comes to steal, kill and destroy. I've come to give you life and give you life abundantly."* It's in the same verse: steal, kill and destroy, and abundant life. We're living on the abundant life side, and we're opposing the steal, kill, and destroy side. We shouldn't move away from the abundant life. Yes, we can be empathetic. Yes, we can be wanting to take swarms of people with us. But we shouldn't lose the joy of living in abundance.

We did not shelter in place just to say, "I'm never going to come out." What happened in 1 Kings 17 is when the prophet Elijah had gone and was living at the brook Cherith and was getting water during a time of drought from the brook and the ravens were feeding him, eventually the scripture says, "And then the brook dried up." God will sometimes use circumstances to move us into the next phase of our living with Him. As we go forward the key differentiator is His presence. The cloud is an invitation to a new way of living, not a temporary day cover or night light. The principle of the cloud is: move with the cloud. Every time the cloud moved, they moved. They didn't know whether the cloud would hover for 10 minutes or for 10 months. They didn't know whether they'd be in a place for two days or for two years, but they had to keep their eye on the cloud.

The same is true for our business. We need to keep our eye on the cloud of God above our business which shelters us; it's our UV protection during the day and the pillar of fire is our warmth by night, our light by night. When it moves, day or night, we move with the cloud. We can live post-corona, but we should never live post-cloud.

I therefore pray as you go forward in your business and grab the initiative that you would say, "God, may your presence be with me. Otherwise, how will they know that you sent me? May your signs and wonders, confirm the words that you've given me. May your presence, your glory, be in my products, in my processes, in everything that I do. May your truth be in my foundations. And may I carry the presence of God into this new season. May I be a person who preserves capital, a person who takes others with me, a person who appreciates your daily provision, but has an eye on the Promised Land where in that land we will plant, we will harvest, we will build barns, we will create wealth and we will create a model of what it is you want for your people here on earth."

God bless you as you go forward. Thank you for going through these 50 principles with me.

A final reminder that you can go to http://brettjohnson.biz/podcast to get this series and others like it in an audio format. I trust these principles have been instructive and encouraging to you. God bless you. And thank you for reading the book.

Testimonials from the rēStart Class

"This feels like the future of the church!" —*Andrew*

"During this lockdown period I was trying to pray and think a lot. But reStart gave me a structure for faith, trusting God in all these different things. It gave me a lot of clarity in this time in planning for the business going forward." —*Andries*

"It's played a significant role in activating how I collaborate with God and move forward in faith into the marketplace with a viable business." —*Chloe*

"It's all starting to come together and taking me literally from the desert into the Promised Land in such a short period of time." —*Debbie*

"I have met some wonderful people and hopefully will have a lasting relationship." —*Denise*

"Things have already started to move and shift in my life. I am no longer fearful of the future. I have an incredible hope. I am so excited for the future and post lockdown coronavirus economy." —*Dirk*

"I realized that I needed something like this to break into my life and get my attention. It's been life-changing. It's definitely changed my perspective and made me very hungry to collaborate with God in everything I do." —*Tim*

"reStart has been a real eye opener in many ways for me. It has helped me to know that He still continues to give creative ideas and do miracles in the marketplace." —*Alex*

"When I think of reStart: renewed, refocused, challenged, empowered, grace given, God-given prophetic insights, and hard work rewarded." —*Hillary*

"I feel that [reStart] gives me the space and grace to fight some personal giants. Having space to do this gives me my joy back." —*Shirleen*

"I think being an entrepreneur can be very lonely. You are always in the muck and mire. It's a reminder that we're all in this together and that God is with us." —*John*

"reStart has pushed me to really think about my responsibility and accountability for facing the giants. Is life all about me? Is it all about money? About being first? I believe God wants me to rebuild, revive, and restore meaningful livelihoods. I want to raise up Kingdom entrepreneurs. I want to coach and disciple." —*Brian*

"Partnering with your spouse is beautiful and challenging at the same time. That is my biggest learning." —*Joe*

"reStart has definitely been a thumbs up in terms of hope, faith, courage, and encouragement." —*Alex*

"The Lord has given me back my voice to be who He has called me to be." —*Denise*

"I am hearing from God differently." —*Debbie*

"Through this class I have learned to allow the Lord to give me a paradigm shift in whatever areas I need, where I am not thinking the way He thinks." —*Denise*

"These are such unusual times. It's heightened for me the need for this kind of community where we can process, pray, and align our businesses with God's Kingdom principles." — *Chloe*

"It's powerful! So encouraging and confidence building." — *Susan*

"It brought more clarity to me for God's purpose for my life and He actually took me to a new level of impact." — *Francois*

"I feel envisioned, equipped, and encouraged!" —*Chloe*

"I can feel how God is working very specifically in my life." — *Dirk*

"It's helping me reset and reframe my thinking and thought processes in so many ways. My decision-making processes have gotten clearer and easier." —*Jackie*

"Being right there in the middle of the workday brings a great reminder and a bridge to a different Kingdom." — *Andrew*

"The material is extremely ordered. It's order and faith. Now I can trust God for my product, my purpose, positioning and presence." —*Andries*

"The biggest takeaway I received from reStart has been that I am a co-collaborator with God and He really wants me to work alongside with Him, not just for him, in accomplishing His Kingdom purposes." —*John*

"reStart has helped me to reframe, not just my business but all areas of my life." —*Felicia*

"Practical business benefit can emerge from me being made over, renewed, and challenged by God, resulting in new confidence in who God has made me to be and to know and document more succinctly and clearly what I am about and what God is about." —*Hillary*

"Even though I've always spoken about integrating business with the Gospel and equipping people, I never saw it so practically done." —*Tim*

Can I just say what I really appreciated about everything that you've done is this: I love the super-pro way that you've presented it. This is pretty much the way business schools present their stuff. So, it really is A Class. I appreciate the fact that you document what you believe and yet, at the same time... you have included the fact that all of us see "through a glass darkly" and I think the humility and maturity required to do that... I appreciate that a lot.—*Rai*

I wanted to share something from the rēp alumni perspective, having taken the core rēp Training about five times, and I've been on five different ventures in different countries, including the U S. What did I get out of it? I got even more out because [when you are serving on a Venture] you're always thinking about your client and, and praying for miracles for your client and less inwardly focused. I wasn't thinking about me and my business and my purpose statement. So rēStart gave me the space to really focus on what I lay into the next stage of my career, and how do I think about the nations? How do we think about discipling others? It's just more practical, I think, for those who've taken it before. —*Amy*

"It's been so encouraging to hear other people and other entrepreneurs struggle with how to integrate faith and work, and know that we're all on this journey together." —*John*

I have loved getting reunited with alumni. I feel like this has been a water table rising, like I've needed my water table to be lifted. I've just loved being with you and God's word. The word is so faithful that things that you have heard before are refreshed or revived or exposed in new ways, just depending on the circumstances. And for me, I came into this really looking to kind of get a restart on a particular purpose that I feel like God birthed in Shawn and I a long time ago, not knowing that we would actually walk out our purpose for a period of time, which we have, and that was a huge blessing. But also just having refreshment around and conviction on my day to day, the stuff that I do all day, every day with my team, with the people I work with, that's been massively encouraging and challenging. And so I just feel boosted in all areas. —*Jodene*

Appreciate the language. I think coming out of the church and work situation that I was in before, just the statement you made this morning about "grace without truth is sloppy and truth without grace is harsh" is just such a big deal. Because I often look at church situations and I think, man, I just want the people of God to be as efficient as possible for the mission that we've been given, and you want to put people in a good position. You want people to run fast, and you don't want anything to be in the way. And I have been in so many different situations where there's a lot of grace but everything's really sloppy, and it's never really clicked with me. I want people to be efficient, everybody to have their role ... And I feel like this course has helped with that language to transcend from my working environment to the church environment.—*Jono*

Books by the author

Brett and Lyn Johnson are the founders of The Institute for Innovation, Integration & Impact, Inc, which was founded in the San Francisco Bay Area / Silicon Valley in 1996. Passionate about the abolition of dichotomy——eradicating the false barriers between facets of life, Brett is particularly interested in removing the barrier between the so-called secular and sacred. A father, writer, and social entrepreneur, Brett is dedicated to societal transformation through business, capital and leadership. Brett has over forty years of experience with leading public accounting and management consulting firms. Brett holds a Bachelor of Commerce degree from the University of Cape Town, and is a Chartered Accountant (C.A., S.A.) He worked at PWC for 14 years, and was a partner at KPMG Peat Marwick and Computer Sciences Corporation.

Born and raised: Cape Town, South Africa. Lyn and Brett met when they were seven years old and married in 1979. They have four children and three grandchildren, all in the USA. They split their time between the USA and Africa.

Brett has authored a variety of books and has a weekly blog and podcast which you can find at
http://brettjohnson.biz

1. Convergence—Integrating your Career, Community, Creativity & Calling
2. I-Operations—How the Internet can transform your Operating Model with Gary Daichendt, former EVP of Worldwide Operations at Cisco
3. LEMON Leadership—Radically fresh leadership
4. Repurposing Capital—Rediscovering Faith-based Financing
5. Transforming Society—A framework for fixing a broken world
6. CYCLES—A journey to Purpose
7. 50 Principles of faith-based financing
8. X-Ordinary—The amazing stories of ordinary people in business with God
9. The Initiative Index—What women wish men knew about the signals men send
10. The Availability Index—What men wish women knew about the signals women send
11. LEMON for Lovers
12. Repurposing People
13. 10 Steps to Restoration
14. rēStart: Reset your foundations for a fresh future

The rēStart Class outline

These are some of the topics that were tackled in the rēStart Class.
https://www.brettjohnson.biz/restart

- Assessing Reality: where is your business right now?
  - Kingdom Business Assessment
  - When is a business dead?
  - What do you have in your hands?
- Finding opportunities without being opportunistic
  - Speaking to dry bones, "Come alive, come alive"
  - Seeing the wells
  - Sowing in famine
  - Calling things that are not as though they are
- Pruning and Pressing: discerning the difference
  - Identifying and Cutting off dead wood
  - Pruning the fruitful branches
  - Pressing the fruit (surrendering what should be crushed)
- Purpose: reconsidering a high-impact, kingdom-focused purpose statement in light of the global epidemic
  - Crisis Impact Assessment
- Prophecy: dusting off prophecies, relating to prophets, seeking fresh words
- Foundational Principles: inspecting your own foundations
  - Identifying cracks in your foundations
  - Demystify the confusion between Values and Foundational Principles
  - Resetting the ancient stones, restoring old walls, building new cities
- Shifting to Promised Land Economics

- o   Three Economic Systems
- Ways in which God repurposes: seeing the fingerprints of God in your life in this crisis
- Households: rethinking your scope of responsibility
  - o   In times of crisis
  - o   In times of plenty
- Making disciples through business: how to integrate disciple-making into core business processes
- God's glory in business: how to anticipate, cast vision for and plan to see God's glory manifest in all of The 10-Ps (10 drivers of organizational impact)

Contact us
info@inst.net

You can also find out more about the author at
http://about.me/thebrettjohnson

Key websites
https://brettjohnson.biz
http://inst.net
http://repurposing.biz
http://lemonleadership.com
http://heartistry.info

www.ingramcontent.com/pod-product-compliance
Lightning Source LLC
Chambersburg PA
CBHW050509210326
41521CB00011B/2383